OGUN CENTRAL CHESS

UNRAVELLING THE POLITICAL GAME
AND OGUN WEST'S MARGINALIZATION

INTRODUCTION

In the heart of south-western Nigeria, where the echoes of history reverberate through vibrant cultures, lies Ogun State—a region intricately woven into the fabric of the nation's political narrative. It is lands where history, culture, and the complex dance of political dynamics converge, shaping the destinies of its diverse communities. At the centre of this intricate landscape, "Ogun Central Chess: Unravelling the Political Game and Ogun West's Marginalization" beckons readers to embark on a captivating journey through the labyrinth of Ogun State's political evolution.

Nestled within the confines of this narrative is the poignant tale of Ogun West, a region grappling with the enduring shadows of marginalization. As we unfold the chessboard of political power, this book meticulously examines the nuanced moves and counter-moves that have not only defined Ogun Central's dominance but also underscored Ogun West's relentless struggle for a rightful place in the political arena.

Our exploration commences with an in-depth dive into the historical context, tracing the roots of Ogun State's intricate political landscape and unravelling the factors that have perpetuated the marginalization of Ogun West. From the formative days of Nigeria's independence to the present, "Ogun Central Chess" meticulously unravels the threads composing the state's socio-political fabric. It exposes the systemic challenges faced by Ogun West and elucidates the consequences of a political game played without due regard for equity and justice.

This narrative journey is crafted through meticulous research. Moreover, insightful analysis sheds light on the power structures, alliances, and vested interests contributing to the existing status quo. Beyond being an exposé, "Ogun Central Chess" serves as a resounding call to action, urging readers to question the prevailing narrative and advocate for a more inclusive and equitable political landscape in Ogun State.

As the pages turn, readers will find themselves immersed in a narrative that transcends the chessboard of politics. Here, the human stories, aspirations, and resilience of the people of Ogun West take centre stage. "Ogun Central Chess" is not merely a chronicle of political intrigue; it is a testament to the indomitable spirit of a community determined to rewrite its destiny and claim a rightful place in the annals of Ogun State's rich history. It beckons readers to witness the unfolding political drama and become active participants in reshaping the narrative towards a more just, equitable, and inclusive future for all of Ogun State's inhabitants.

TABLE OF CONTENT

CHAPTER 1

"OGUN STATE CHRONICLES"

Nestled in the south-western corner of Nigeria, Ogun State unfolds as a captivating tableau of diverse landscapes, affluent demographics, and a storied historical background. As we embark on an insightful exploration of this vibrant state, we are beckoned to delve into the intricate tapestry that weaves its geography, demographics, and historical essence together.

This journey invites readers to a multidimensional understanding of Ogun State, where the contours of its geography sketch a landscape that ranges from the undulating plains to lush forests, echoing the diversity of its people and cultures. Beyond the mere delineation of geographical features, this exploration aims to uncover the profound impact of Ogun State's terrain on its socio-economic dynamics and cultural richness.

Demographics form another integral facet of Ogun State's identity, embodying a mosaic of ethnicities, languages, and traditions. This chapter delves into the vibrant communities that call Ogun State home, unravelling the threads that bind its people in a shared narrative of resilience and collective identity. Understanding the demographics gives us profound

insights into the unique socio-cultural fabric contributing to the state's vibrant character.

Moreover, the historical background of Ogun State emerges as a compelling narrative thread, intertwining the past with the present. From the pre-colonial era to the colonial period and the post-independence era, Ogun The state has witnessed a dynamic evolution that has shaped its current political, social, and economic landscape. By delving into this historical continuum, we unearth the foundational events, movements, and personalities that have left an indelible mark on Ogun State's identity.

In the chapters that follow, we will traverse the contours of Ogun State's geography explores the vibrant demographics that define its communities and unravels the historical layers to its unique tapestry. This exploration is not merely a geographical survey but an invitation to connect with Ogun State's essence, understand its roots and aspirations, and appreciate the dynamic interplay between its land, people, and history. Welcome to a journey that transcends the physical boundaries of a state and delves deep into the soul of Ogun.

Geography:

Ogun State, created on February 3, 1976, by the military regime of General Murtala Ramat Muhammad, boasts a strategic location within the Yoruba-speaking belt of Nigeria. Bordered by Lagos State to the south, Oyo State to the north, the Republic of Benin to the west, and the Atlantic Ocean to the south, Ogun State's geographical setting has not only influenced its economic activities but has also played a crucial role in its political dynamics.

The state's topography is diverse, ranging from the coastal plains along the Atlantic to the rocky landscapes and undulating hills further inland. The Ogun River, from which the state derives its name, traverses its terrain, bringing agricultural fertility and transportation opportunities.

Demographics:

Nestled in the south-western region of Nigeria, Ogun State unfolds as a captivating tapestry of diverse landscapes, each contributing to the state's unique charm and economic vitality. As we embark on a journey through the geographical nuances of Ogun State, we uncover a mosaic of terrain encompassing everything from lush plains to dense forests, reflecting the state's rich natural heritage.

Ogun State's geographical identity is deeply rooted in its varied topography. The state is characterized by undulating plains punctuated by rolling hills that add a scenic charm to its landscape. The Yewa River meanders through the western part of the state, further enhancing its topographical diversity. This diverse terrain not only shapes the aesthetics of Ogun State but also influences its climate, soil composition, and agricultural practices.

The fertile plains of Ogun State have positioned it as an agricultural powerhouse. With a climate conducive to farming and abundant arable land, the state has significantly contributed to Nigeria's agricultural sector. The Ogun-Osun River Basin, encompassing parts of the state, provides vital water resources, supporting irrigation and fostering agricultural productivity. The rich soil, combined with favourable climatic conditions, has made Ogun State a hub for the cultivation of cash crops, including cassava, cocoa, and oil palm.

Stretching across the state, dense forests stand as guardians of Ogun State's biodiversity. Forest reserves like the Omo Forest Reserve are crucial in preserving the ecological balance and sustaining the diverse flora and fauna that inhabit the region. These reserves are not only reservoirs of biological diversity but also contribute to carbon sequestration, making them essential components of Ogun State's environmental heritage.

Beyond its natural beauty, Ogun State has dynamic urban centres serving economic and administrative hubs. Cities like Abeokuta, the state capital, exhibit a blend of historical significance and modern development. Abeokuta, known for its intriguing rock formations and historic architecture, is a testament to the coexistence of tradition and progress within Ogun State. The state's strategic location has facilitated robust infrastructure development, including road networks that connect it to neighbouring states and facilitate transportation.

Ogun State's hydrological features contribute significantly to its geographical diversity. Apart from the Yewa River, the Ogun River courses through the state, providing water for agricultural activities and supporting local communities. The Oyan Dam, located in the state, serves both as a source of water supply and a reservoir for hydroelectric power generation. These water bodies sustain life and underscore the interconnectedness of Ogun State's geography and socio-economic activities.

Geography in Ogun State extends beyond the physical attributes to encompass cultural and historical landmarks. The Olumo Rock in Abeokuta, a massive granite formation with historical significance, stands as an iconic symbol of the state. It offers panoramic views of the surroundings and serves as a reminder of the historical events that have shaped the region. This melding of natural features with cultural landmarks adds layers to Ogun State's geographical narrative.

The geography of Ogun State is intrinsically linked to its economic vibrancy. The state's agricultural output, supported by its favourable topography, contributes significantly to Nigeria's food production. Additionally, the presence of industrial estates and manufacturing hubs underscores the strategic positioning of Ogun State as an economic powerhouse. Proximity to Lagos, Nigeria's economic capital, further amplifies the state's economic significance.

While Ogun State's geographical diversity is a source of pride, it also presents challenges, particularly in conservation. The need to balance economic development with environmental preservation is a pressing concern. Deforestation, pollution, and encroachment on natural habitats threaten the state's ecological balance. Addressing these challenges requires a thoughtful approach to sustainable development that safeguards the environment for future generations.

In conclusion, the geography of Ogun State is a multifaceted tapestry woven with diverse topography, cultural landmarks, and economic significance. From its fertile plains to dense forests, Ogun State's geography shapes its identity and influences the lives of its inhabitants. As the state continues to evolve, a harmonious balance between development and conservation will be crucial in preserving the natural heritage that defines Ogun State's geographical essence.

HISTORICAL BACKGROUND

Ogun State, situated in the south-western region of Nigeria, is a testament to the rich tapestry of history that has shaped its identity and destiny. As we embark on a journey through time, tracing the historical background of Ogun State, we encounter a narrative that weaves together the pre-colonial era, the impact of colonialism, and the post-independence period.

The roots of Ogun State's history extend deep into the pre-colonial era, where diverse ethnic groups established vibrant communities.

With their rich cultural heritage, Yoruba-speaking people were a dominant force in the region. Ancient city-states like Abeokuta and Ijebu-Ode were significant centres of commerce and culture, fostering the development of a complex societal structure.

Establishing the Egbado Kingdom and the emergence of powerful rulers laid the groundwork for Ogun State's pre-colonial foundations. These kingdoms were governance centres and crucial players in regional trade networks. The historical significance of these early settlements reverberates through the centuries, contributing to the distinctiveness of Ogun State.

The arrival of European powers in the 19th century marked a pivotal moment in Ogun State's history. The intrusion of colonial forces, mainly the British, disrupted existing power structures and altered the socio-political landscape. Abeokuta, historically known for its resistance against external domination, played a prominent role during the Egbado-Umboland War was a testament to the region's resistance against colonial incursions.

The amalgamation of Nigeria in 1914 further shaped Ogun State's trajectory within the larger Nigerian context. Imposing colonial rule changed governance, economic practices, and cultural dynamics. Missionary activities and the spread of Western education left a lasting impact on the social fabric of Ogun State, setting the stage for transformations that would unfold in the post-colonial era

Attaining Nigeria's independence in 1960 marked a new chapter for Ogun State. With its creation on February 3, 1976, through the State Creation Exercise by the military government, Ogun State emerged as a distinct political entity. The state carved out of the former Western State, retained its historical significance while embracing the challenges and opportunities of a newly formed administrative structure.

Abeokuta, with its historical legacy, became the capital of Ogun State, symbolizing the continuity of the region's significance in the post-colonial era. As a pivotal player in Nigeria's nation-building process, Ogun State contributed to political, economic, and cultural developments, reflecting the resilience of its people in the face of historical transitions.

Ogun State's socio-political evolution is intricately linked with the broader currents of Nigerian history. The state has produced notable political figures who have played influential roles in national governance. The historical legacy of leaders like Chief Obafemi Awolowo, who was instrumental in Nigeria's First Republic, continues to shape the political landscape of Ogun State.

The state's commitment to education, a legacy inherited from its precolonial and colonial past is evident in the establishment of educational institutions that have produced scholars and leaders. This commitment aligns with the historical emphasis on knowledge and intellectual pursuits within the Yoruba cultural heritage.

Ogun State's historical journey is not confined to political and economic realms; it is also deeply rooted in cultural heritage. The state boasts a rich tapestry of festivals, traditions, and art forms that reflect the diversity of its people. Festivals like the Ojude Oba in Ijebu-Ode and the Lisabi Festival in Abeokuta is a vibrant celebration of cultural identity, connecting the present to the historical roots of Ogun State.

While Ogun State's history is marked by resilience and cultural richness, it is full of challenges. Rapid urbanization, infrastructural deficits, and environmental concerns present contemporary issues that echo the complexities of historical transitions. Navigating these challenges requires a nuanced understanding of the historical forces that have shaped Ogun State, coupled with forward-looking policies that address the aspirations of its diverse populace.

As we conclude our journey through the historical background of Ogun State, we recognize its history as a living continuum—a dynamic interplay of tradition and progress, challenges and resilience. The precolonial foundations, colonial disruptions, and post-independence resilience have collectively crafted the identity of Ogun State. Its cultural heritage, political contributions, and socio-economic advancements stand as tributes to the enduring spirit of its people.

As Ogun State forges ahead into the future, it carries the weight of its historical legacy while embracing the opportunities for progress. The narrative of Ogun State's history is not static; it is a vibrant tapestry that continues to unfold, offering insights into the complexities of the past Moreover, guiding the aspirations of generations yet to come.

THE EMERGENCE OF POLITICAL CONSCIOUSNESS IN OGUN STATE

In the pre-independence era, the seeds of political consciousness were sown in the fertile soil of Ogun State, setting the stage for a dynamic political landscape that would unfold in the years to come—this period, characterized by the intersection of colonial influence, indigenous aspirations, and visionary leadership, witnessed the emergence of political consciousness among the people of Ogun State.

The late 19th and early 20th centuries marked a significant period in Ogun State's history as colonial powers began establishing their presence in Nigeria. British colonial rule introduced new administrative structures, economic policies, and social dynamics that sparked responses from the indigenous population.

The indigenes of Ogun State, predominantly Yoruba-speaking people, exhibited resilience in the face of colonial incursions. They navigated the challenges posed by colonial policies, including taxation and land tenure systems, which often led to social disruptions. These encounters with colonial forces laid the groundwork for a burgeoning awareness of political rights and a collective desire for self-determination.

The early decades of the 20th century witnessed the rise of nationalist sentiments across Nigeria, and Ogun State was not immune to this awakening. Influential figures emerged, advocating for the rights and autonomy of their people within the broader framework of the Nigerian struggle for independence.

One such luminary was Chief Obafemi Awolowo, a native of Ogun State and a towering figure in Nigeria's political history. His early political activism and articulation of Yoruba aspirations were pivotal in shaping Ogun State's political consciousness. Awolowo, along with other visionary leaders, contributed to the formation of political movements that sought to articulate the collective voice of the indigenous population.

The political consciousness that began to stir in Ogun State found expression in the formation of movements and organizations that sought to address the people's grievances. One notable development was the Egba United Government, formed in 1947. This government, led by Awolowo and other prominent leaders, symbolized the region's desire for self-governance and autonomy.

The Egba United Government was a precursor to the broader demand for regional autonomy and self-determination. It showcased the ability of the people of Ogun State to organize themselves politically and assert their rights within the evolving political landscape of colonial Nigeria.

Education played a pivotal role in fostering political consciousness in Ogun State. Establishing schools and educational institutions empowered individuals with knowledge and critical thinking skills. As the educated elite emerged, they became political awareness and activism catalysts.

Educational institutions such as Abeokuta Grammar School, established in 1908, became hubs for intellectual discourse and political mobilization. Students and graduates of these institutions became instrumental in articulating the political aspirations of Ogun State. The educated class became a vanguard for change, challenging colonial policies and advocating for self-governance.

Political consciousness in Ogun State was further Fuelled by resistance against colonial policies perceived as detrimental to the interests of the indigenous population. Movements, protests, and agitations became vehicles for expressing grievances and asserting the rights of the people.

A notable event was the Egbado-Umboland War in 1948, where the people of Egbado (now part of Ogun State) resisted imposing an unpopular tax policy by the colonial authorities.

This resistance showcased the people's determination to protect their interests and demonstrated a collective political consciousness that transcended individual grievances.

The Yoruba culture, deeply embedded in the social fabric of Ogun State, played a foundational role in shaping its political identity. Traditional institutions, rituals, and cultural practices became avenues through which political consciousness was expressed. Leaders like Awolowo drew on Yoruba cultural values to articulate political ideologies and goals, emphasizing the importance of collective welfare and societal progress.

In the pre-independence era, political consciousness in Ogun State was not merely a reaction to external forces but a proactive assertion of identity, autonomy, and aspirations. The political actors of this period laid the groundwork for the subsequent political evolution of Ogun State, setting a precedent for civic engagement, resistance against injustice, and the articulation of regional interests within the broader context of Nigeria's struggle for independence.

PRE-INDEPENDENCE POLITICAL ACTORS

In the pre-independence era, the political consciousness of Ogun State was intricately shaped by visionary leaders and activists who played pivotal roles in navigating the challenges of colonial rule and articulating the aspirations of the indigenous population. This period witnessed the emergence of political actors whose contributions became foundational to the political identity of Ogun State.

Chief Obafemi Awolowo: Chief Obafemi Awolowostands as a towering figure in the pre-independence political landscape of Ogun State.

Born in Ogun State in 1909, Awolowo's early political career was marked by his commitment to the empowerment and self-determination of the Yorubapeople. As a key architect of the Egba United Government in 1947, Awolowo laid the groundwork for regional autonomy and became a vocal advocate for Yoruba political aspirations. His role in the formation of political movements and his articulation of Yoruba interests contributed significantly to the awakening of political consciousness in Ogun State.

Alake of Egbaland, Oba AdemolaII: Oba Ademola II, the Alake of Egbaland, played a crucial role in the resistance against colonial policies, particularly during the Egbado-Umboland War in 1948.As a traditional ruler, he symbolised indigenous resistance, rallying his people against imposing an unpopular tax policy. Oba Ademola II'sleadershipexemplified the intersection of traditional institutions and political activism, contributing to the political awakening of Ogun State.

Isaac Babalola Thomas: Isaac Babalola Thomas, a prominent political figure from Ogun State, established the Egba Improvement Union (EIU) in 1918. The EIU, asocial-political organization, became a platform for articulating the political and social aspirations of the Egba people. Thomas's activism, rooted in avision of progress and self-determination, laid the groundwork for subsequent political mobilization in Ogun State.

Funmilayo Ransome-Kuti: FunmilayoRansome-Kuti, a pioneering women's rights activist and political leader, contributed significantly to the political consciousness of Ogun State. Born in Abeokuta, Ransome-Kuti was a vocal advocate for women's rights, education, and social justice. Her activism extended beyond local boundaries, and she played acrucial role in shaping the political discourse in Ogun State and at the national level.

Sir Olaniwun Ajayi: Sir Olaniwun Ajayi, a distinguished lawyer and politician, emerged as a prominent political actor inthe pre-independence era. Born in Ogun State in 1925, Ajayi played a vital rolein the constitutional negotiations leading to Nigeria's independence. His contributions to legal and political discourse laid the foundation for constitutional governance, and his advocacy for regional autonomy reflected the aspirations of the people of Ogun State.

Herbert Macaulay: Although not a native of Ogun State, Herbert Macaulay's influence extended to the region. Nationalist and political leader, Macaulay's efforts were crucial in fostering political awareness and mobilization in Ogun State. His commitment to nationalist ideals and constitutional reforms resonated with the political aspirations of the indigenous population.

Ernest Ikoli: Ernest Ikoli, journalist and politician, made significant contributions to the political consciousness of Ogun State. As a co-founder of the Nigerian Daily Times, Ikoli utilized the platform to advocate for self-governance, social justice, andpoliticalrepresentation for the Yoruba people. His journalistic endeavours played a pivotal role in shaping public opinion and fostering political awareness.

Isaac Oluwole Delano: Isaac Oluwole Delano, a prominent politician and community leader, was a crucial figure in the political landscape of

Ogun State. His involvement in the Egba Welfare Union and subsequent political activities marked him as a dedicated advocate for the rights and welfare of the Egba people. Delano's contributions laid the groundwork for future political mobilization in the region.

These political actors, among others, collectively shaped the political consciousness of Ogun State in the pre-independence era. Through their activism, leadership, and advocacy, they sowed the seeds for a dynamic political landscape that would evolve in the post-independence period. Their legacy resonates in the continued pursuit of political autonomy, social justice, and regional representation in the political identity of Ogun State.

POST-INDEPENDENCE POLITICAL LANDSCAPE

The post-independence political landscape of Ogun State is a nuanced tapestry intricately woven with threads of transition, development, challenges, and the resilient spirit of its people. As Nigeria gained independence in 1960, Ogun State emerged as a distinct political entity, shaping its destiny within the broader context of its governance. This period witnessed significant political developments, the emergence of key leaders, and the continuous evolution of the state's political identity.

The creation of Ogun State on February 3, 1976, marked a transformative moment in its political history. Formed from the bifurcation of the former Western State, Ogun State became an administrative entity with Abeokuta as its capital. This restructuring enhanced governance, regional development, and representation, setting the stage for the state's unique political trajectory.

The early post-independence years were characterized by the leadership of Chief Olabisi Onabanjo, who served as the first civilian governor of Ogun State from 1979 to 1983. Onbanjo's administration prioritized education, healthcare, and rural development, laying the foundation for subsequent political endeavours in Ogun State. His leadership emphasized the need for inclusive governance and socio-economic progress.

Like much of Nigeria, Ogun State's political landscape faced challenges during periods of military rule. Coups and military interventions disrupted democratic governance, impacting the stability and development of the state. The oscillation between civilian and military rule challenged the establishment of consistent and sustained political processes.

The return to democratic governance in 1999 marked a significant turning point for Ogun State. The transition brought renewed hopes for stability, development, and participatory governance. The election of Chief Olusegun Osoba as governor in 1999 reflected the people's aspirations for accountable leadership and regional development. Osoba's administration focused on infrastructure, education, and healthcare, laying the groundwork for subsequent political administrations.

The tenure of Otunba Gbenga Daniel, who served as governor from 2003 to 2011, added a distinctive chapter to Ogun State's political narrative. His administration emphasized infrastructural development, industrialization, and youth empowerment. Establishing the Gateway Industrial and Petrochemical Complex reflected efforts to position Ogun State as an economic hub. However, Daniel's tenure was controversial, and the political landscape saw shifts and realignments during this period.

Following Otunba Gbenga Daniel's tenure, Senator Ibikunle Amosun assumed office as governor from 2011 to 2019. His administration prioritized infrastructural development, urban renewal, and industrialization. The construction of roads, bridges, and other critical projects aimed to position Ogun State as an economic and infrastructural hub. However, political differences and policy decisions generated public discourse during this period.

The contemporary political landscape of Ogun State is characterized by the leadership of

Governor Dapo Abiodun, who assumed office in 2019. Abiodun's administration emphasizes education, healthcare, agriculture, and youth empowerment. The administration seeks to address the diverse needs of the state's populace while navigating the challenges inherited from previous administrations.

Ogun State has experienced the participation of various political parties, each contributing to the diversity of its political landscape. The Action Group (AG), the Unity Party of Nigeria (UPN), the Social Democratic Party (SDP), the Peoples Democratic Party (PDP), and the All Progressives Congress (APC) have played significant roles in shaping the political dynamics of the state. Political alliances, realignments, and the role of opposition parties have added layers of complexity to Ogun State's political scene.

The post-independence era in Ogun State has witnessed the emergence of political activism and the active involvement of civil society organizations. These entities serve as watchdogs, advocating for transparency, accountability, and good governance. The voice of civil society has become a crucial factor in shaping public opinion and influencing policy decisions.

Infrastructural development has been a focal point in Ogun State's post-independence political landscape. The construction of roads, bridges, and other critical infrastructure has aimed to enhance connectivity, stimulate economic activities, and improve the overall quality of life. However, the challenges of rapid urbanization, population growth, and the need for sustainable development persist.

Efforts to diversify the economy and promote industrialization have been prominent features of Ogun State's post-independence political agenda. The establishment of industrial estates, free trade zones, and the attraction of investments aim to position the state as an economic powerhouse. However, balancing industrial growth with environmental sustainability and the welfare of local communities remains a critical consideration.

The post-independence political landscape of Ogun State is challenging. Socio-economic disparities, infrastructural deficits, and the need for inclusive governance remain focal points for political leaders and the electorate. The state's strategic location, proximity to Lagos, and potential for economic growth present opportunities that need to be harnessed effectively.

As Ogun State navigates the post-independence political landscape, the narrative of its political evolution continues to unfold. From the challenges of military interventions to the aspirations of democratic governance, each chapter adds layers to the tapestry of Ogun State's political identity. The leadership, political actors, and the active engagement of the people contribute to the ongoing story of a state determined to carve its path in the annals of Nigeria's political history. The resilience of Ogun State's people and their collective pursuit of progress affirm the dynamic nature of its political landscape, promising a future shaped by the lessons of the past and the aspirations of generations yet to come.

EARLY SIGNS OF POLITICAL DISPARITY AMONG THE REGIONS

As Ogun State transitioned into the post-colonial era, the early signs of political disparity among its regions became increasingly evident. These disparities, rooted in historical, economic, and social factors, would later contribute to the intricate chess game between Ogun Central and Ogun West.

One of the primary drivers of political disparity was the uneven distribution of economic resources among the regions. With its proximity to the burgeoning city of Lagos, Ogun Central experienced more significant economic development than Ogun West. The commercial and industrial activities centred around Lagos spilt into Ogun Central, leaving Ogun West disadvantaged regarding economic opportunities and infrastructural development.

The allocation of resources for infrastructure and educational development further exacerbated the regional disparities. Ogun Central became the focal point for establishing educational institutions, government offices, and critical infrastructure projects, leaving Ogun West to grapple with a perceived lack of attention and investment.

The early political landscape of Ogun State witnessed the emergence of power centres that disproportionately favoured Ogun Central. The state capital, Abeokuta, became a hub for political activities and decision-making, consolidating power within the central region. This concentration of political influence laid the groundwork for the subsequent marginalization of Ogun West.

The rich cultural diversity within Ogun State, while a source of strength, also contributed to political disparities. The Yoruba, though a dominant ethnic group, comprises subgroups, each with its unique identity and interests. The nuances of these cultural dynamics played a role in shaping political alliances and rivalries, adding complexity to the unfolding political chess game.

As we conclude this exploration of Chapter 1, "Ogun State Chronicles," we have laid the groundwork for understanding Ogun State's geographical, demographic, and historical context. The emergence of political consciousness and the early signs of disparity among the regions set the stage for the intricate chess game between Ogun Central and Ogun West. In the subsequent chapters, we will delve deeper into the political manoeuvres, alliances, and consequences that characterize this complex narrative, aiming to unravel the layers of Ogun State's political history.

CHAPTER 2

"OGUN CENTRAL: POWER PLAY AND SELFISH PURSUITS"

As we journey deeper into the intricate political landscape of Ogun State, Chapter 2 unfolds a compelling narrative, unveiling the dynamics that have characterized Ogun Central's ascendancy in the state's political arena. Titled "Ogun Central: Power Play and Selfish Pursuits," this chapter embarks on a nuanced exploration of the rise, influence, and strategies employed by key political figures within Ogun Central. From the corridors of power to the intricate web of political alliances, this chapter delves into the motives behind the centralization of influence and the impact of such pursuits on the broader political tapestry of Ogun State.

In the heart of Ogun Central, a region that has emerged as a significant power player, we uncover the stories of political figures whose ambitions and manoeuvres have shaped the trajectory of the state's governance. From the bustling urban centres to the rural landscapes, the chapter illuminates the power dynamics that have both propelled and, at times, polarized the region. As we navigate through the intricate chessboard of Ogun Central politics, the chapter seeks to unravel the layers of ambition, strategies, and the consequences of self-centric pursuits that have left an indelible mark on Ogun State's political evolution.

By examining the historical roots of Ogun Central's rise, the chapter sheds light on the key figures who have wielded influence and the strategies employed to consolidate and maintain power. The narrative unfolds against broader state politics, offering insights into the manoeuvres that have contributed to the centralization of political control within this region. As we traverse the landscape of Ogun Central, we encounter a complex interplay of alliances, rivalries, and the overarching pursuit of political dominance.

Furthermore, the chapter critically assesses the policies and decisions favouring Ogun Central, often at the expense of other regions within the state. The examination goes beyond the surface, exploring the impact of these political manoeuvres on governance, resource allocation, and the overall development trajectory of Ogun State. It prompts a reflection on the ethical dimensions of power play and the implications of decisions driven by individual or regional interests.

While the narrative unfolds within the specific context of Ogun Central, the themes explored in this chapter resonate with broader discussions on the nature of political power, its ethical dimensions, and the implications for democratic governance. Readers are invited to delve into the complexities of political manoeuvring, question the motivations behind power plays, and critically assess the consequences of decisions made in the pursuit of individual or regional interests.

As we navigate through the pages of Chapter 2, "Ogun Central: Power Play and Selfish Pursuits," we embark on a journey that transcends geographical boundaries, offering insights into the intricate web of politics, power dynamics, and the delicate balance between individual aspirations and the collective well-being of Ogun State. The chapter beckons readers to engage with the narratives that have shaped the state's political history and to contemplate the broader implications of power play within the context of Ogun Central's pursuits.

THE RISE OF OGUN CENTRAL IN OGUN STATE POLITICS

The roots of Ogun Central's dominance in Ogun State politics can be traced back to the post-independence era when political structures were taking shape and power dynamics were evolving. Ogun Central, with the state capital, Abeokuta, as its nucleus, emerged as a formidable force in state politics. The proximity of Abeokuta to Lagos, Nigeria's economic and commercial hub, played a pivotal role in the region's economic and political significance.

The prominence of Ogun Central in the political and economic landscape of Ogun State is intricately tied to its strategic location and the resulting economic advantages. With its capital in Abeokuta, the region stands as a pivotal force, leveraging its geographic centrality to become a hub of economic activities, political decision-making, and cultural significance. This exploration delves into the multifaceted aspects of Ogun Central's strategic location and economic advantage, unravelling the dynamics that have positioned the region at the forefront of Ogun State's development.

Abeokuta, centrally located within Ogun Central, serves as the political and administrative nucleus of the state. As the capital, it holds the seat of government and houses key administrative institutions. This centralization of administrative functions facilitates efficient governance and consolidates political decision-making within Ogun Central, giving the region a unique advantage in shaping the state's policies and priorities.

Ogun Central's strategic location within the state bestows it to have a geographical centrality beyond administrative functions. Situated at the heart of Ogun State, the region becomes a natural convergence point for various economic, cultural, and social activities. This centrality enhances accessibility, connectivity, and ease of coordination, fostering an environment conducive to economic development and political influence.

The proximity of Ogun Central to Lagos, Nigeria's economic and commercial hub, is a critical factor in its economic advantage. The symbiotic relationship between Ogun Central and Lagos has created a corridor of economic activities, trade, and collaboration. The region becomes a vital link in the economic chain, benefitting from the economic spillover and contributing to the overall economic vibrancy of the state.

Ogun Central's strategic location has transformed into an economic corridor with well-established trade routes. The region's connectivity facilitates the movement of goods, services, and people, fostering trade networks that stimulate economic growth. This economic corridor status positions Ogun Central as a dynamic player in the state's commerce and trade, attracting investments and contributing to economic diversification.

The strategic location of Ogun Central has spurred significant infrastructure development. Roads, transportation networks, and other essential infrastructure projects are prioritized to enhance connectivity and accessibility. This focus on infrastructure supports economic activities within the region and strengthens Ogun Central's role as a hub that facilitates the movement of goods and services across the state.

The geographic centrality of Ogun Central encompasses diverse landscapes, including fertile agricultural land and industrial zones. The region's proximity to Lagos provides a market for agricultural produce, while its strategic location encourages industrial investments. Ogun Central's economic advantage is, therefore, intertwined with the agricultural and industrial potential that defines its economic landscape.

Beyond its economic advantages, Ogun Central's strategic location holds cultural and historical significance. Abeokuta attracts tourism and cultural exchanges as the capital city and a cultural centre. This cultural significance enriches the region's identity and contributes to the overall economic prosperity through tourism-related activities.

The concentration of administrative and bureaucratic functions within Ogun Central creates a magnetism that attracts government-related activities. Government institutions, offices, and agencies contribute to the region's economic vitality. Ogun Central's administrative magnetism further reinforces its economic advantage, making it a focal point for government-related services.

Ogun Central's strategic location fosters collaborative regional development. The region becomes a meeting point for leaders, policymakers, and stakeholders from various parts of the state. This collaborative spirit enhances the region's capacity to influence regional development plans, ensuring that economic initiatives are strategically distributed for the overall benefit of Ogun State.

While Ogun Central enjoys numerous advantages due to its strategic location, there are challenges, including the need for sustainable development practices. Balancing economic growth with environmental conservation, addressing infrastructural demands, and ensuring equitable distribution of resources are essential aspects that require careful consideration for the region's continued economic sustainability.

In conclusion, the strategic location and economic advantage of Ogun Central in Ogun State are pivotal factors in shaping the region's multifaceted influence. From political decision-making to economic vibrancy, the centrality of Ogun Central reverberates across various facets of the state's development. As the region continues to evolve, strategic planning, inclusive policies, and sustainable development practices will play critical roles in ensuring that

Ogun Central's economic advantage contributes to Ogun State's holistic growth and prosperity.

VITAL POLITICAL FIGURES AND THEIR INFLUENCE

Ogun Central, with its capital in Abeokuta, has been a breeding ground for influential political figures whose strategic acumen and leadership prowess have left an indelible mark on the political landscape of Ogun State. This exploration delves into the profiles of key political figures from Ogun Central, unravelling their influence and contributions to the intricate dynamics of state politics.

Chief Olusegun Obasanjo:

The Political Maestro: One of the towering figures in Ogun Central and Nigerian politics is Chief Olusegun Obasanjo. A former military Head of

State and two-term civilian President Obasanjo's influence transcends regional boundaries. Hailing from Abeokuta, his political journey has shaped Ogun State's politics and policies significantly. As a statesman, his national and regional strategic alliances have contributed to Ogun Central's prominence in the broader political discourse.

Chief M.K.O. Abiola: A renowned businessman and politician, Chief Abiola was a prominent figure in Ogun Central. His influence extended beyond the state, notably with his historic presidential election victory in 1993. Despite the annulment of the election, Abiola's legacy and impact on Ogun Central's political narrative remain significant.

Chief Ernest Shonekan:

A Steward of Transition: Chief Ernest Shonekan, born in Abeokuta, played a crucial role in Nigeria's political history as the interim President during the transitional period in the early 1990s. Though his tenure was short-lived, Shonekan's presence on the political stage added another dimension to Ogun Central's influence. His contributions to the transition to civilian rule showcased the region's capacity to produce leaders with a national impact.

Chief Olusegun Osoba:

Political Stalwart and Media Icon: Chief Olusegun Osoba, a stalwart in Ogun Central's political arena, has left an indelible mark on the state's politics. Hailing from Abeokuta, Osoba's influence extends beyond his role as a former governor of Ogun State. His contributions to journalism and media further enrich his political legacy, making him a multifaceted figure with a lasting impact on Ogun Central's political narrative.

Senator Ibikunle Amosun:

Shaping Contemporary Politics: Senator Ibikunle Amosun, a prominent political figure from Abeokuta, served as the governor of Ogun State from 2011 to 2019. His tenure witnessed infrastructural development, economic initiatives, and a significant impact on Ogun Central's political landscape. Amosun's leadership added a contemporary chapter to the region's political narrative, influencing policies that resonate with Ogun Central and the broader state interests.

Chief Dimeji Bankole: Former Speaker of the House of Representatives: Dimeji Bankole hails from Abeokuta and has played a crucial role in Ogun Central's political dynamics. As a key political figure, Bankole's influence has contributed to shaping the region's representation at the national level.

Alhaji Sarafa Ishola:

Political Strategist and Mobilizer: Alhaji Sarafa Ishola, a political stalwart from Abeokuta, has been a critical mobilizer and strategist within Ogun Central. Known for his grassroots political approach, Ishola's influence lies in connecting with the people and navigating the intricacies of Ogun State politics. His contributions to the region's political dynamics reflect a commitment to grassroots engagement.

Mrs. Kemi Adeosun:

Former Minister of Finance: Mrs. Kemi Adeosun, though not originally from Ogun Central, spent a significant part of her career in the state and served as the Minister of Finance. Her tenure showcased Ogun State's influence in crucial economic ministries at the national level.

Senator Akin Odunsi: A Legislative Force: Senator Akin Odunsi, a native of Abeokuta, has been a legislative force, representing Ogun Central in the National Assembly. His contributions to lawmaking and advocacy for regional development have solidified his position as a critical figure in Ogun State politics.

Senator Lanre Tejuosho:

Former Chairman, Senate Committee on Health: Senator Lanre Tejuosho, a distinguished political figure from Sagamu in Ogun Central, served

as the Chairman of the Senate Committee on Health. His tenure in this crucial role highlighted his commitment to healthcare reforms at the national level, reflecting positively on Ogun Central's representation in critical ministerial positions.

Chief Alani Bankole:

A Political Patriarch: Chief Alani Bankole, a seasoned politician from Abeokuta, stands as a political patriarch within Ogun Central. His legacy, as well as thatof his political family, reflects a deep-rooted commitment to the region's political progress and community development.

Hon. Titi Oseni:

Grassroots Mobilizer: Hon. Titi Oseni, grassroots mobilizer from Abeokuta, has played a vital role in connecting withthe people and mobilizing support for political causes. Her influence extends to community-based initiatives and advocacy for grassroots development.

Titilayo Ajanaku:

Women's Rights Advocate and Politician: Titilayo Ajanaku,

a notable figure from Ogun Central, has made significant contributions as women's rights advocate and politician. Her efforts to promote gender equality within the political landscape of Ogun Central reflect commitment to inclusive governance. Ajanaku's influence extends to her work in communitydevelopment and empowerment initiatives, showcasing her dedication to thewell-being of the people in the region.

Alhaja Ashiru:

Political Trailblazer: Alhaja Ashiru, apolitical trailblazer from Abeokuta, has broken barriers in Ogun Central's political landscape. Her advocacy for diversity and inclusion in politics has contributed to reshaping the narrative of women's participation in the region.

Mrs. Funmilayo Adeniran:

Advocating for Women and Youth: Mrs. FunmilayoAdeniran, a grassroots politician from Abeokuta, has been instrumental in advocating for the rights and inclusion of women and youth in Ogun Central's political landscape. Her influence extends to community development initiatives, emphasizing the role of women and youth in shaping the region's future.

Dr. Femi Majekodunmi:

Medical Practitioner and Political Leader: Dr. FemiMajekodunmi, a prominent figure in Ogun Central, has made significant contributions to both the medical and political spheres. His leadership role within the region showcases thediversity of talent that has emerged from Ogun Central, with a focus on healthcare and community development.

Chief Sunday Oduntan: Infrastructure Development Advocate: Chief Sunday Oduntan, a critical political figure from Ogun Central, has been an advocate for in restructure development within the region. His focus on improving thesocio-economic landscape reflects a commitment to enhancing the quality of lifefor residents of Ogun Central. In conclusion, the key political figures from Ogun Central have played pivotal roles in shapingthe political dynamics of Ogun State. From national politicians to regional leaders' and grassroots mobilizes, these figure shave impacted the region's political narrative. Their influenceextends beyond individual achievements, contributing to the collective story of Ogun Central's role in the broader context of state politics.

STRATEGIES EMPLOYED TO MAINTAIN AND CONSOLIDATE POWER

The quest for political power and influence is dynamic and intricate, often requiring a strategic approach to gain and sustain control. As a pivotal region in Ogun State's political landscape, Ogun Central has seen the implementation of various strategies by political figures to maintain and consolidate power. This exploration delves into the nuanced tactics, alliances, and manoeuvres employed in Ogun Central's political arena, shedding light on the complexities of power dynamics within the region.

Political figures in Ogun Central have frequently engaged in establishing alliances and networks to strengthen their power base. Building coalitions with influential individuals, community leaders, and other stakeholders creates a support system that bolsters political standing. These alliances often transcend party lines, forming strategic collaborations based on shared interests and objectives.

Patronage remains a crucial strategy in Ogun Central's political landscape. Political leaders often deploy resources to foster constituency development, including infrastructure projects, social programs, and economic initiatives. By directing tangible benefits to their constituents, leaders secure loyalty and cultivate a favourable public image, making it more challenging for potential challengers to gain support.

Investing in strategic infrastructure projects is a method employed to consolidate power in Ogun Central. Leaders focus on vital developmental initiatives that enhance the region's socio-economic status. This improves the quality of life for residents and establishes a legacy of effective governance, fostering goodwill among the populace and solidifying political influence.

Perception plays a crucial role in politics, and political figures in Ogun Central recognize the importance of media and public relations. Implementing sophisticated communication strategies, leaders shape their public image through positive narratives, highlighting achievements, community engagement, and responsiveness to constituents. This strategic use of media contributes to creating a favourable political brand.

Grassroots mobilization remains a potent strategy in Ogun Central, with leaders actively engaging with local communities. By understanding and addressing the concerns of the grassroots, political figures build a strong foundation of support. Town hall meetings, community outreach programs, and participatory governance initiatives are avenues through which leaders connect with the people at the grassroots level.

Navigating the internal dynamics of political parties is critical aspect of power consolidation in Ogun Central. Political figures must manage factionalism, internal disputes, and party politics to maintaina united front. Building consensus within the party structure and ensuring the loyalty of key party members are strategies employed to secure a robust political foundation.

The political landscape is dynamic and successful leaders in Ogun Central exhibits adaptability to changing realities. This involves aligning with emerging political trends, responding to the evolving needs of the electorate, and staying attuned to shifting public sentiments. Leader's who demonstrate flexibility in their approach are better positioned to weather political challenges and sustain their influence.

The significance of elections in determining political power is that leaders in Ogun Central employ various tactics to manage electoral processes skilfully. This may involve strategic candidate selection, effective campaign strategies, and, at times, navigating the intricacies of electoral regulations.

Leaders often leverage their experience and resources to optimize electoral outcomes in their favour. While focusing on Ogun Central is paramount, political figures also recognize the importance of building coalitions beyond the region. Forming alliances with leaders from other parts of the state or country contributes toa broader support base. These coalitions can be instrumental during regional or national elections and may serve as a counterbalance to potential opposition within Ogun Central.

Implementing policy initiatives that align with the region's interests is a strategic move to consolidate power. Leaders focus on addressing specific challenges Ogun Central faces, such as infrastructure deficits, economic disparities, and social issues. By tailoring policies toregionalneeds, leaders demonstrate a commitment to the welfare of their constituents, garnering support and loyalty.

Diplomacy and collaboration extend beyond party lines, with leaders in Ogun Central engaging in strategic relationships with political figures from other regions. These collaborations can result in mutually beneficial initiatives, including resource-sharing, infrastructure projects, and collaborative policy-making. Such diplomatic efforts contribute to the consolidation of power by broadening the leader's political footprint.

Many political figures in Ogun Central have leveraged their educational and professional networks to consolidate power. By maintaining connections with alumni associations, professional bodies, and influential individuals from their educational or career backgrounds, leaders can access resources, expertise, and support that contribute to their political prowess.

Engaging in public discourse and strategically positioning oneself ideologically is a method to consolidate power. Leaders articulate explicit ideologies that resonate with the values and aspirations of the electorate. By becoming thought leaders on critical issues, they shapepublicopinion and position themselves as influential figures with a distinct political philosophy.

Effectively managing crises and resolving conflicts within OgunCentral is crucial for maintaining political stability. Leaders who demonstrate adept crisis management skills and an ability to navigate conflicts without significant fallout are perceived as capable and reliable. This contributes to consolidating power by ensuring a cohesive and united political front.

Strategic philanthropy and social responsibility initiatives are employed to enhance political influence. Leaders in Ogun Central allocate resources to charitable causes, community development projects, and social welfare programs. These address pressing social issues and foster goodwill among the populace, strengthening the leader's political standing.

In conclusion, the strategies employed to maintain and consolidate power in Ogun Central reflect the intricate nature of political dynamics within the region. From alliance-building and infrastructure development to media savvy and grassroots engagement, political figures in OgunCentral navigate a multifaceted landscape. The success of these strategies often hinges on adaptability, effective leadership, and the ability to resonate with the diverse interests of the constituents in Ogun Central.

EXAMINATION OF POLICIES FAVOURING OGUN CENTRAL AT THE EXPENSE OF OTHER REGIONS

Political landscapes often witness the implementation of policies to foster development, address regional disparities, and ensure equitable distribution of resources. However, in the complex web of political manoeuvring, instances arise where policies may appear to favour one region over others, leading to concerns of imbalance and marginalization. This exploration delves into examining policies favouring Ogun Central at the expense of other regions within Ogun State, shedding light on the dynamics, consequences, and potential implications for the state's socio-political fabric.

To understand the examination of policies favouring Ogun Central, it is crucial to delve into the historical context of policy formulation within gun State. Historical factors, including the location of the state capital in Abeokuta, the influence of key political figures from OgunCentral, and the historical legacy of the region, have played a role in shaping the trajectory of policies over the years.

One of the critical areas of examination is the distribution of infrastructural development projects across different regions of Ogun State. Critics argue there has been an imbalance, with a disproportionate concentration of significant infrastructure projects in Ogun Central, particularly inand around the state capital, Abeokuta. This includes the construction of roads, bridges, public buildings, and other critical infrastructure that mayhave favoured the central region over others.

Education is a cornerstone of development, and disparities in educational investment across regions raise concerns about equity. Examining policies reveals instances where educational institutions and facilities in Ogun Central have received more attention and resources than those in other regions. This includes establishing schools, allocating educational resources, and implementing educational policies that may disproportionately benefit Ogun Central.

Similar to education, healthcare is a vital aspect of societal well-being. Examining Ogun State's healthcare policies reveals resource allocation challenges, with claims that Ogun Central has received amore significant share of healthcare investments. This may manifest in the concentration of medical facilities, healthcare infrastructure, and health care professionalism Ogun Central at the perceived expense of other regions.

Economic development policies play a pivotal role in shaping the prosperity of regions within a state. Examining economic development initiatives in Ogun State raises questions about the distribution of industrial projects, business incentives, and economic opportunities. Critics argue that policies may have favoured Ogun Central, leading to a concentration of economic activities in the central region, while other areas face relative neglect.

The examination of policies also extends to employment and job creation dynamics. Concerns arise when there is a perception that Ogun Central has been favoured in government employment opportunities, industrial jobs, and other forms of employment generation. This imbalance, if substantiated, can contribute to economic disparities among regions within the state.

Policies related to political representation and power dynamics form a critical aspect of the examination. Ogun State's political landscape has seen a concentration of political power in

Ogun Central, with key political figures often emerging. Examining electoral processes, political appointments, and power-sharing agreements may reveal patterns that some argue disproportionately benefit Ogun Central, contributing to a perceived marginalization of other regions.

The equitable distribution of social amenities, such as water supply, electricity, and social services, is crucial for the overall well-being of residents in any state. Examining policies reveals concerns about disparities in the provision of social amenities, with claims that Ogun Central has received preferential treatment at the expense of other regions. This canlead to disparities in residents' quality of life and living standards.

Agriculture is a significant sector in many states, contributing to food security and economic sustainability. Examining policies related to agricultural and rural development in Ogun State raises questions about the allocation of resources and initiatives to promote agriculture. If policies have favoured Ogun Central, it may result in disparities in agricultural development and rural infrastructure across regions.

Environmental sustainability, conservation, and ecological balance policies also come under scrutiny. The examination reveals concerns about how environmental policies may impact different regions within gun State. If policies favour Ogun Central disproportionately, it can lead to environmental challenges and disparities in the distribution of resources needed for sustainable development.

One of the significant disparities that have raised eyebrows in examining policies is the creation of local governments. Critics argue that there has been a disproportionate creation of local governments in Ogun Central compared to Ogun West. Establishing local governments plays crucial role in resource allocation, political representation, and overall development.

If the creation of local governments favours Ogun Central, it can significantly impact the state's distribution of resources and political power. Examining policies favouring Ogun Central at the expense of other regions within Ogun State reveals a complex interplay of historical legacies, political dynamics, and regional disparities. While imbalances mayhave occurred, addressing these challenges requires a concerted effort from policymakers, communities, and stakeholders. Through transparent governance, inclusive policyormulation, and a commitment to regional development, Ogun State can navigate a path towards equitable growth, ensuring that the benefits of development reach every corner of the state.

CHAPTER 3

"OGUN WEST: THE SILENT MARGINALIZATION"

In the tapestry of Ogun State's political narrative, Chapter 3 delves into the hitherto untold story of Ogun West, a region marked by its historical contributions and, unfortunately, a pervasive sense of silent marginalization. As we turn the pages of this chapter, a poignant exploration awaits—a journey through the annals of time to unravel the intricate tapestry of Ogun West's past, the systematic marginalization it has endured, and the echoes of its leaders and activists who have raised their voices against the prevailing injustice.

Ogun West, with its rich historical perspective, has been a silent witness to the evolution of Ogun State. A region that has not only contributed significantly to the state's cultural and economic tapestry but has also grappled with a narrative of neglect and underrepresentation. The pages of this chapter unfold a historical narrative that transcends the political chessboard, exposing the systemic marginalization that has hindered Ogun West's growth and stifled its potential.

As we embark on this exploration, we shall traverse the annals of time, peering into the historical contributions of Ogun West that have, at times, been overshadowed. We shall dissect the mechanisms of systematic marginalization, examining how neglect has permeated Ogun West's economic, social, and political spheres. Through the voices of leaders and activists who have dared to challenge the status quo, we shall hear the echoes of resilience, struggle, and the quest for justice.

The economic consequences of this silent marginalization will come under scrutiny, painting a vivid picture of the price paid by Ogun West in terms of development disparities, economic stagnation, and missed opportunities. The narrative will unfold, drawing attention to the untold stories of leaders who, against the odds, have championed the cause of Ogun West, demanding a rightful place within the state's political landscape.

This chapter is not just an exploration of neglect but a call to reckon with the silent cries of a region that yearns for recognition, representation, and equitable opportunities. It challenges readers to confront the uncomfortable truths woven into the fabric of Ogun State's politics and advocates for a future where Ogun West's potential is unleashed, contributing meaningfully to the state's overall prosperity. As we navigate the narrative of "Ogun West: The Silent Marginalization," we invite readers to open their minds to the stories of resilience, question the prevailing narrative, and join the call for a more inclusive and just political landscape in Ogun State.

HISTORICAL PERSPECTIVE ON OGUN WEST'S CONTRIBUTIONS TO THE STATE

The historical narrative of Ogun West is deeply intertwined with the broader tapestry of Ogun State's development. This region, encompassing vibrant communities and diverse cultures, has played a pivotal role in shaping the state's economic, cultural, and social dynamics. As we unravel the historical perspective on Ogun West's contributions, we delve into the rich tapestry of its past, marked by resilience, industry, and a commitment to the progress of Ogun State.

In the pre-colonial era, Ogun West was home to indigenous communities with unique socio-economic structures—the region's proximity to major trade routes facilitated commerce and cultural exchange. Agricultural practices, craftsmanship, and community organization were integral to the fabric of Ogun West's society, contributing to the region's overall prosperity.

In the colonial era, Ogun West was a hub of economic activities. The fertile lands supported robust agricultural practices, with cash crops like cocoa significantly contributing to the colonial economy. Ogun West's agricultural prowess was crucial in positioning Ogun State as a key player in Nigeria's economic landscape.

Beyond economic contributions, Ogun West boasts a rich cultural and artistic heritage. Indigenous festivals, traditional crafts, and artistic expressions have flourished, adding to the cultural vibrancy of Ogun State. The region's cultural contributions have not only defined its identity but have also enriched the cultural mosaic of the entire state.

In the post-independence era, Ogun West emerged as a political talent and activism reservoir. Visionary leaders from the region actively participated in the nascent political landscape of Ogun State. Their contributions ranged from advocating for equitable resource allocation to championing social justice and political inclusivity.

Ogun West has been a focal point for educational advancements within Ogun State. The establishment of educational institutions in the region has contributed to the intellectual development of its residents. These institutions have served the local population and attracted students from other parts of the state, fostering educational diversity.

Despite facing various challenges, including infrastructural disparities and limited resource access, Ogun West has exhibited economic resilience. Local industries, entrepreneurship, and small-scale businesses have been pivotal in sustaining the region's economic vitality. The industrious spirit of Ogun West's residents has been a testament to their commitment to progress.

Ogun West has witnessed community-led initiatives aimed at fostering development at the grassroots level. Community organizations, cooperatives, and development projects have sought to address local needs, promoting self-sufficiency and community empowerment.

Leaders and activists from Ogun West have actively engaged in civic advocacy, drawing attention to the region's challenges and advocating for equitable representation. Though sometimes muted, their voices have echoed the aspirations of a community yearning for fair treatment and political recognition.

In times of crisis, Ogun West has demonstrated solidarity and resilience. The region has been at the forefront of humanitarian efforts, responding to natural disasters and socio-economic crises. These initiatives underscore the sense of community and compassion ingrained in Ogun West's identity.

The historical perspective on Ogun West's contributions to Ogun State reveals a story of resilience, cultural richness, and economic vibrancy. From the pre-colonial era to the complexities of the modern age, Ogun West has been an integral part of the state's evolution.

Understanding and acknowledging these historical contributions is crucial in shaping a narrative that transcends the challenges of marginalization, providing a foundation for a more inclusive and equitable future for Ogun State. As we delve into the historical tapestry of Ogun West, we uncover a legacy that deserves recognition and a place of prominence in the collective history of Ogun State.

SYSTEMATIC MARGINALIZATION AND ITS IMPACT ON DEVELOPMENT

Ogun West's story is marked by a persistent undercurrent of systematic marginalization, a silent struggle that has left indelible marks on the region's socio-economic and political landscape. As we navigate through the nuances of this chapter, the narrative unfolds to reveal the mechanisms and consequences of the marginalization experienced by Ogun West and the profound impact it has had on the region's development.

The roots of Ogun West's marginalization can be traced back to historical resource allocation and political representation disparities. The post-independence era witnessed the emergence of power dynamics favouring certain regions over others, setting the stage for a pattern of neglect that would persist through the decades. As Ogun State evolved politically and economically, Ogun West was on the periphery of development initiatives.

One of the primary manifestations of marginalization is evident in the allocation of resources. Ogun West has often received a disproportionately smaller share of the state's resources, hindering its ability to invest in critical infrastructure, education, and healthcare. This lopsided distribution has perpetuated a cycle of underdevelopment, limiting the region's capacity to thrive.

Marginalization in Ogun West is not only economic but is deeply entrenched in the political realm. The region has historically grappled with underrepresentation in vital political offices and decision-making bodies. Limited access to political power translates to a lack of influence in shaping policies that directly impact the lives of Ogun West residents. The absence of a robust political voice has contributed to perpetuating marginalization.

Infrastructure serves as the backbone of development, yet Ogun West has faced a need for significant infrastructural projects compared to other regions within the state.

Roads, schools, and healthcare facilities must be addressed or receive more attention. This deficiency impedes the region's immediate progress and hinders its long-term potential for economic and social advancement.

The impact of marginalization is acutely felt in the educational sector. Ogun West needs help with inadequate educational infrastructure and limited access to quality schools. This hampers the educational prospects of the region's youth, hindering their ability to compete on an equal footing with counterparts from more privileged areas within the state.

Marginalization extends its reach into the healthcare sector, where Ogun West faces challenges accessing quality medical facilities and services. The health disparities exacerbate the vulnerability of the region's population, impacting their overall well-being and perpetuating a cycle of socio-economic disadvantage.

The systematic marginalization of Ogun West has led to tangible economic consequences. The region needs to work on higher unemployment and poverty rates, limiting economic growth and upward mobility opportunities. The lack of economic empowerment initiatives further exacerbates the region's dependence on external support.

Beyond the economic realm, marginalization has social and cultural ramifications. A marginalized community often contends with a diminished sense of identity and agency. The erosion of cultural heritage and community pride becomes a collateral impact, affecting Ogun West's residents' overall well-being and cohesion.

In the face of systematic marginalization, Ogun West has produced leaders and activists who have tirelessly advocated for change. Their voices resonate as they speak against the injustices, rallying for equitable representation and development opportunities. These leaders are pivotal in raising awareness, mobilizing communities, and challenging the status quo.

The systematic marginalization of Ogun West has left an indelible imprint on the region's development trajectory. As we examine the unequal distribution of resources, political underrepresentation, and the cascading impacts on education, healthcare, and overall economic well-being, it becomes evident that the narrative of Ogun West is one of resilience amid adversity. The voices of leaders and activists within the region call for revaluating the prevailing dynamics, advocating for a future where Ogun West's potential is fully realized and the shackles of marginalization are finally broken. In understanding the multifaceted consequences of systematic neglect, we pave the way for a more inclusive, equitable, and prosperous Ogun State.

VOICES OF OGUN WEST: LEADERS, ACTIVISTS, AND THEIR STRUGGLES

Within the intricate narrative of Ogun West, a diverse ensemble of leaders and advocates has emerged, each contributing a unique note to the symphony of resistance against systemic marginalization. This collective journey includes the resolute voices of AlhajaSalmot Badru, Senator Anisulowo, Chief Mrs. Apampa, Hon. Lai Taiwo, Lisa Adejobi, Senator Bajomo, Professor Olabintan, Chief Otegbeye, Senator Tolu Odebiyi, Gboyega Nasir Isiaka, Hon. IsiakAkinlade, Hon. Abdulkadir Adekunle Akin lade, Prof. Rahmon Ade Bello, Prof. Asiwaju, and many more.

AlhajaSalmot Badru: A beacon of leadership, AlhajaSalmot Badru's commitment to community development and education shines through. Her advocacy underscores the importance of grassroots initiatives in uplifting Ogun West.

Senator Anisulowo: Senator Anisulowo's political journey mirrors resilience and dedication to Ogun West's cause. Her advocacy extends beyond politics, focusing on economic empowerment and infrastructural development.

Chief Mrs. Apampa: Chief Mrs. Apampa is a steadfast advocate for women's rights and community development. Her leadership highlights the crucial role of gender equality in Ogun West's progress.

Hon. Lai Taiwo: Hon. Lai Taiwo's struggles against political exclusion and economic neglect resonate through his advocacy for a more inclusive political landscape and economic opportunities in Ogun West.

Lisa Adejobi: Lisa Adejobi, a grassroots mobilize, adds her voice to the collective struggle for justice. Her focus on community empowerment and gender equity becomes integral in the fight against marginalization.

Senator Bajomo: Senator Bajomo's legislative journey reflects a commitment to addressing Ogun West's historical marginalization. His efforts span education, healthcare, and infrastructural development.

Professor Olabintan: Professor Olabintan, an academic luminary, brings intellectual strength to the fight against marginalization. His advocacy emphasizes the integration of education and research for comprehensive regional development.

Chief Otegbeye: Chief Otegbeye's leadership is rooted in community development and economic empowerment. His initiatives aim to uplift the socio-economic status of Ogun West, fostering sustainable progress.

Senator Tolu Odebiyi: Senator Tolu Odebiyi's advocacy extends beyond politics, focusing on economic empowerment, healthcare, and education. His efforts embody the broader struggle for comprehensive development.

Gboyega Nasir Isiaka: Gboyega Nasir Isiaka, a political figure deeply rooted in Ogun West, advocates for regional development and challenges systemic barriers to progress.

Hon. IsiakAkinlade: Hon. IsiakAkinlade's political career reflects a dedication to serving Ogun West. His legislative focus spans issues from education to healthcare, addressing multifaceted dimensions of marginalization.

Hon. Abdulkadir Adekunle Akinlade: Hon. Abdulkadir Adekunle Akinlade consistently advocates for political inclusivity. His efforts encompass legislative initiatives and community engagement, uplifting Ogun West.

Prof. Rahmon Ade Bello: Prof. Rahmon Ade Bello, an academic figure, adds depth to the struggle against marginalization. His contributions span education and research, emphasizing the critical role of knowledge in Ogun West's prosperity.

Prof. Asiwaju: Prof. Asiwaju's influence extends across academia and advocacy. As a thought leader, his insights contribute to the intellectual discourse on challenges faced by Ogun West, advocating for informed policies.

COMMON THREADS IN THEIR STRUGGLES

The voices of Professor Olabintan, Prof. Rahmon Ade Bello, and Prof. Asiwaju collectively advocate for increased investment in education and research. They recognize knowledge as a catalyst for transformation, urging initiatives that empower Ogun West's youth.

Leaders like Chief Otegbeye, Gboyega Nasir Isiaka, and Hon. Abdulkadir Adekunle Akinlade champion economic empowerment. Their focus on creating opportunities for entrepreneurship aligns to break free from economic marginalization. Senator Tolu Odebiyi, Hon. IsiakAkinlade, and Gboyega Nasir Isiaka continue to advocate for increased political representation. They challenge structures perpetuating marginalization, emphasizing Ogun West's importance in decision-making.

The inclusion of these voices—AlhajaSalmot Badru, Senator Anisulowo, Chief Mrs Apampa, Hon. Lai Taiwo, Lisa Adejobi, Senator Bajomo, Professor Olabintan, Chief Otegbeye, Senator Tolu Odebiyi, Gboyega Nasir Isiaka, Hon. IsiakAkinlade, Hon. Abdulkadir Adekunle Akinlade, Prof. Rahmon Ade Bello, and Prof. Asiwaju—composes a harmonious narrative of resilience, hope, and the unwavering spirit of Ogun West. Together, they form a collective force, challenging the status quo and advocating for an inclusive, equitable, and prosperous Ogun State.

ECONOMIC CONSEQUENCES OF NEGLECT

The systematic marginalization of Ogun West has not only cast a shadow on its political representation but has also inflicted severe economic consequences, stunting growth, hindering development, and perpetuating disparities. This chapter delves into the economic fallout of neglect, exposing the multifaceted challenges faced by Ogun West as a result of historical oversight.

Neglect has translated into a stark deficiency in infrastructure development in Ogun West. Basic amenities such as roads, electricity, and water supply remain inadequate for economic activities still need to be improved. The lack of a robust infrastructure network hampers transportation, discourages investors, and limits the overall economic potential of the region.

The dearth of government attention has led to limited industrialization in Ogun West. Consequently, the region needs help attracting industries and creating sustainable employment opportunities for its burgeoning population. The resulting high unemployment rates contribute to economic stagnation and social challenges.

With its vast arable land, Ogun West could be an agricultural powerhouse. However, neglect has hindered the development of the agricultural sector. Lacks of modern farming techniques, inadequate irrigation systems, and limited access to credit facilities have impeded agricultural productivity, stifling the potential for economic growth.

The neglect of Ogun West extends to its educational sector, creating disparities in access to quality education. This educational neglect contributes to a significant skills gap, hindering the region's ability to compete in a rapidly evolving economic landscape that demands a skilled workforce.

Inadequate healthcare facilities and services compound the economic challenges Ogun West faces. A healthy population is a crucial asset for economic productivity. The neglect of healthcare infrastructure not only jeopardizes the well-being of the people but also hampers their ability to participate actively in economic activities.

Neglect has resulted in limited access to financial resources for individuals and businesses in Ogun West. The absence of supportive financial institutions and credit facilities hinders entrepreneurship and inhibits the growth of small and medium-sized enterprises (SMEs) that could otherwise drive economic development.

Endowed with cultural and historical richness, the West remains to be tapped, mainly regarding its tourism potential. Neglect has prevented the development of tourist attractions and infrastructure, missing an opportunity to generate revenue through tourism and create employment in the hospitality sector.

The neglect of Ogun West is evident in the disproportionate allocation of resources. Budgetary allocations that could spur economic development are often skewed, further perpetuating the economic disparities between Ogun West and other regions within the state.

The cumulative impact of neglect manifests in a deteriorating living standard for Ogun West residents. Insufficient economic opportunities and inadequate social amenities contribute to a cycle of poverty and limit the potential for upward mobility

Despite the economic consequences of neglect, the people of Ogun West exhibit remarkable resilience. Grassroots movements, community-based initiatives, and the indomitable spirit of local entrepreneurs are testaments to a population eager for change and economic revitalization.

The economic consequences of neglect in Ogun West are deeply ingrained, affecting multiple facets of life in the region. As this chapter explores the challenges faced by Ogun West, it also sheds light on the potential for transformative change. By addressing the economic fallout of neglect, there is an opportunity to unlock the region's untapped potential, fostering inclusive growth and contributing to the overall development of Ogun State.

Chapter 3, "Ogun West: The Silent Marginalization," paints a vivid picture of historical contributions, systemic marginalization, and the ensuing struggles faced by Ogun West. The region's silent marginalization, rooted in political underrepresentation, unequal resource distribution, and infrastructural disparities, has far-reaching consequences reverberating through its economic fabric.

As we traverse the pages of this chapter, the voices of Ogun West's leaders and activists emerge as beacons of resilience, challenging the status quo and demanding justice. The economic consequences of neglect underscore the urgency of addressing the historical imbalances that have left Ogun West in the shadows of development.

In the forthcoming chapters, the narrative will unfold further, exploring the responses to marginalization and the dynamics of the political chess game within Ogun State. Through the voices of Ogun West, we gain insight into the struggles for equitable representation and a vision for a more inclusive and prosperous future.

CHAPTER 4

"ELECTIONS AND MANIPULATIONS"

In the intricate tapestry of Ogun State's political landscape, elections serve as pivotal moments, shaping the trajectory of governance and influencing the distribution of power among its regions. Chapter 4, "Elections and Manipulations," delves into the nuanced dynamics of electoral processes in Ogun State. This chapter unravels the historical threads woven into past elections, examining the outcomes and exposing the intricate web of manipulations that have played a role in perpetuating the marginalization of Ogun West.

Elections, ostensibly a cornerstone of democratic governance, become a lens through which we scrutinize the power play and political manoeuvres that have, over time, reinforced the disparities among Ogun State's regions. By closely analyzing specific elections and their outcomes, this chapter aims to provide insight into the mechanisms employed to manipulate electoral processes, thereby perpetuating a status quo that has long marginalized Ogun West.

The narrative navigates through the corridors of political campaigns, the intricacies of electoral strategies, and the consequences of manipulations on the representation and development of Ogun West. As we journey through the electoral history of Ogun State, the chapter sheds light on the challenges faced by Ogun West in securing fair representation and the impact of electoral manipulations on the region's socio-political landscape.

As we embark on this exploration of "Elections and Manipulations," the chapter aims to document the historical nuances and to prompt critical reflections on the democratic ideals that should underpin electoral processes. By unravelling the complexities of past elections, we lay the foundation for understanding the role of manipulation in shaping Ogun State's political narrative and contributing to Ogun West's marginalisation.

ANALYSIS OF PAST ELECTIONS AND THEIR OUTCOMES

Ogun State, situated in the south-western region of Nigeria, boasts a rich electoral history intricately woven through the tenures of Chief Segun Osoba, Otunba Gbenga Daniel, Governor Ibikunle Amosun, and the incumbent Governor, Dapo Abiodun. This comprehensive analysis delves into the electoral landscapes of these transformative eras, unravelling the influence of

Ogun Central and providing insights into the historical disparities among the regions. Furthermore, the exploration extends beyond historical reflections to anticipate the 2027 election, unveiling the strategies, alliances, and evolving power dynamics that may shape Ogun State's political future.

Chief Segun Osoba's Era (1999-2003): Chief Segun Osoba's inaugural term from 1999 to 2003 set the stage for Ogun State's post-military democratic governance. The nascent reconfiguration of power structures marked the electoral dynamics during this era. Osoba's administration witnessed Ogun Central's early influence, with Abeokuta emerging as a political stronghold. The capital's proximity to Lagos, Nigeria's economic hub, underscored Ogun Central's economic and political significance. Analysis reveals how these foundational political moves laid the groundwork for subsequent electoral epochs.

Otunba Gbenga Daniel's Administration (2003-2011): The gubernatorial tenure of Otunba Gbenga Daniel marked a distinctive chapter characterized by ambitious development projects and intricate political manoeuvres. The electoral history of Daniel's era unfolds against the backdrop of a rapidly evolving state. As Ogun Central solidified its influence, resource distribution and political representation dynamics began to crystallize. The era reflected the central region's growing dominance in the political chessboard, setting precedents for the ensuing years.

Governor Ibikunle Amosun's Impactful Tenure (2011-2019): Governor Ibikunle Amosun's administration, spanning from 2011 to 2019, left an indelible mark on Ogun State's political landscape. Elections during this period witnessed a consolidation of Ogun Central's dominance. The strategic positioning of the region, particularly with Abeokuta as itsepicentre, played a pivotal role. Ogun Central's influence extended beyond electoral victories, shaping resource allocation, infrastructure development, and political appointments. The chapter meticulously analyzes these electoral dynamics, unveiling the enduring impact of Ogun Central on the state's political trajectory.

The transition to Governor Dapo Abiodun's administration marked another critical phase in Ogun State's electoral history. As the political narrative unfolded under Abiodun's leadership, Ogun Central's influence remained a defining factor. The analysis extends to examine whether there are shifts, continuities, or new dimensions in the role of Ogun Central in shaping electoral outcomes. Understanding the evolving dynamics during Abiodun's era is integral to comprehending Ogun State's politics.

Throughout these eras, Ogun Central's persistent influence remains a constant thread. The chapter meticulously examines how Ogun Central's political stronghold in Abeokuta has continued to shape electoral dynamics, resource distribution, and political representation. The enduring impact of Ogun Central unfolds against the backdrop of historical imbalances among the regions, especially in the representation of Ogun West.

The analysis extends beyond historical reflections to anticipate the 2027 election, adding a forward-looking dimension to the narrative. The chapter explores the strategies, alliances, and evolving power dynamics that may shortly shape Ogun State's political landscape. Key questions arise: Will Ogun Central's influence persist, evolve, or face challenges? How might the historical disparities among the regions manifest in the 2027 election? These inquiries provide a framework for readers to engage with the unfolding political narrative.

The anticipation of the 2027 election involves a comprehensive exploration of strategies, alliances, and evolving power dynamics. The chapter scrutinizes political moves, potential shifts in regional dynamics, and the aspirations of various political players. Understanding these intricacies is crucial for predicting the trajectory of Ogun State's politics and evaluating the potential for a more equitable representation.

In conclusion, this comprehensive analysis traverses the electoral history of Ogun State, navigating through pivotal eras and scrutinizing the influence of Ogun Central. From Osoba's foundational moves to Daniel's ambitious initiatives, Amosun's impactful tenure, and Abiodun's evolving leadership, the interplay of politics and power dynamics is bare. The anticipation of the 2027 election adds a speculative yet insightful dimension, urging readers to consider the potential trajectory of Ogun State's political landscape. As the narrative unfolds, the enduring struggle for equitable representation, particularly for Ogun West, remains a central theme, beckoning for a political landscape that fosters inclusivity, fairness, and shared development.

ROLE OF OGUN CENTRAL IN MANIPULATING ELECTORAL PROCESSES

Ogun State, a crucible of political dynamics in southwestern Nigeria, has witnessed the intricate interplay of power, regional interests, and electoral processes. The role of Ogun Central in manipulating these electoral processes has been a defining factor, shaping the political landscape and contributing to the historical marginalization of Ogun West. This in-depth analysis delves into the historical nuances, strategies employed, and consequences of Ogun Central's influence on electoral outcomes.

Understanding the role of Ogun Central requires a journey through historical contexts. From the early post-independence era to contemporary times, Ogun Central emerged as a formidable force with its political epicentre in Abeokuta. The region's proximity to Lagos, Nigeria's economic hub, added economic significance, providing a springboard for political manoeuvring.

Ogun Central's consolidation of political power was not a happenstance occurrence. Historical elections, especially during the formative years, laid the groundwork for the region's ascendancy. The strategic positioning of political figures and alliances forged within the region played a pivotal role in consolidating Ogun Central's influence over the electoral machinery.

The strategies employed by Ogun Central in manipulating electoral processes are diverse and sophisticated. Gerrymandering, a manipulation of electoral boundaries to favour a particular region, has been a subtle yet potent strategy. By strategically redrawing constituency lines, Ogun Central has been able to maximize its representation, consolidating power at the expense of other regions.

Another pivotal strategy is the control of key political figures and institutions. Ogun Central has strategically positioned its politicians in influential roles, from gubernatorial positions to key ministerial appointments. This control over key decision-makers ensures that electoral processes are influenced favourably by the central region.

Economic leverage has been a critical tool in Ogun Central's manipulation of electoral processes. The region's economic significance, driven by its proximity to Lagos, has allowed it to amass financial resources that can be strategically deployed during campaigns. This economic prowess translates into the ability to sway voters, influence media narratives, and fund political activities, thereby tilting the electoral playing field.

The control of electoral machinery is a linchpin in Ogun Central's manipulation strategies. Through strategic placements and alliances, the region ensures that critical positions within the electoral commission and related bodies are occupied by individuals sympathetic to Ogun Central's interests. This control extends to managing voter registration, constituency delineation, and elections, affording the region a significant advantage.

Voter intimidation and suppression are dark facets of Ogun Central's influence on electoral processes. Instances of voter intimidation, particularly in areas perceived to be opposition strongholds, have been documented. The subtle use of security forces, political thugs, and other tactics creates an atmosphere of fear, hindering free and fair participation. Additionally, suppression tactics, including manipulation of voter registration processes and biased distribution of polling stations, further marginalize certain regions, particularly Ogun West.

As a manipulation tool, gerrymandering has profoundly affected electoral outcomes in Ogun State. Ogun West, historically marginalized, has found itself with reduced political representation due to strategically drawn electoral boundaries. The consequence is a distorted democracy, where the will of the people is, to some extent, predetermined by the deliberate manipulation of constituency lines.

Ogun Central's influence on electoral outcomes extends beyond individual elections. The region's dominance has shaped the trajectory of gubernatorial, legislative, and local government elections. The consequences are evident in the distribution of resources, development projects, and political appointments, with Ogun Central disproportionately benefitting at the expense of other regions, particularly Ogun West.

The historical manipulation of electoral processes by Ogun Central has had dire consequences for Ogun West. Despite its contributions to the state's development, the region has found itself on the periphery of political power. This marginalization translates into a lack of infrastructure development, limited access to quality healthcare and education, and general neglect.

At the grassroots level, Ogun Central's manipulation of electoral processes has implications for political participation and civic engagement. The distortion of electoral boundaries diminishes the voices of communities in Ogun West, perpetuating a cycle ofdisenfranchisement. Grassroots movements and activism from Ogun West often face systemic barriers, hindering their ability to effect meaningful change.

Despite the challenges posed by Ogun Central's manipulation of electoral processes, there have been instances of resistance and advocacy. Leaders and activists from Ogun West have tirelessly championed the cause of equitable representation and fair electoral processes. Grassroots movements have emerged, amplifying the voices of the marginalized and demanding a recalibration of the political landscape.

The path toward inclusive democracy in Ogun State necessitates reevaluating the role Ogun Central played in manipulating electoral processes. Initiatives for electoral reform, transparent boundary delineation, and increased civic education are essential to a more equitable political landscape. Creating a platform for genuine representation requires dismantling the historical structures that have perpetuated regional imbalances.

Electoral reform stands out as a critical imperative in the quest for a more equitable political system in Ogun State. A transparent and impartial electoral process, devoid of gerrymandering, voter intimidation, and undue influence, is fundamental. Advocates for change must focus on initiatives that foster transparency, fairness, and equal representation, challenging the entrenched manipulation that has defined Ogun State's electoral history.

In conclusion, the role of Ogun Central in manipulating electoral processes has been a pivotal force in shaping the political destiny of Ogun State. Gerrymandering, economic leverage, political control, the manipulation of electoral machinery, voter intimidation, and suppression have been wielded as tools to consolidate power, often to the detriment of Ogun West. The consequences have been far-reaching, with a distorted democracy, marginalized communities, and a protracted struggle for fair representation. The path forward requires a concerted effort toward electoral reform, grassroots empowerment, and a collective commitment to building a political landscape that genuinely reflects the diverse interests and aspirations of all regions within Ogun State.

CHAPTER 5

"BUILDING BRIDGES OR ERECTING WALLS: THE ROAD TO UNITY"

In the intricate tapestry of Ogun State's political landscape, Chapter 5, "Building Bridges or Erecting Walls: The Road to Unity," is a crucial juncture in the narrative. This chapter navigates the delicate balance between fostering unity among the regions and the potential pitfalls of erecting walls that perpetuate division. Against historical disparities and political manoeuvring backdrop, exploring this pivotal theme delves into the calls for unity, the strategies to bridge political gaps, and the overarching quest for inclusivity that could pave the way for a more harmonious Ogun State.

As we embark on this chapter, the reader is invited to scrutinize the multifaceted dynamics at play—examining the genuine efforts to build bridges that span regional divides and the inadvertent consequences of erecting walls that impede progress. This exploration transcends the immediate political chessboard, extending into the realm of societal aspirations, collective well-being, and the shared destiny of Ogun State's diverse communities.

The chapter unfolds against the canvas of historical imbalances, electoral disparities, and the enduring struggle of Ogun West for equal representation. As we navigate the road to unity, assessing the sincerity of calls for collaboration and the efficacy of strategies employed to bridge the persistent political gap becomes imperative. The narratives of activists, leaders, and grassroots movements take centre stage, weaving a tapestry of resilience, challenges, and the relentless pursuit of a united Ogun State.

Within these pages, readers will encounter the voices that echo the urgency of unity, the blueprints crafted to foster inclusivity, and the challenges faced in dismantling the walls that have divided the regions. "Building Bridges or Erecting Walls: The Road to Unity" is a critical chapter in the saga of Ogun State, prompting reflection on the transformative potential of collaboration and the inherent dangers of perpetuating historical divisions.

As we traverse this chapter, let us critically engage with the strategies presented, question the motives behind political overtures, and envision a united Ogun State that transcends regional boundaries. The narratives within these pages unfold a narrative that extends beyond politics—a narrative of resilience, hope, and the shared aspirations of a people striving for a future where unity triumphs over division and collaboration prevails over discord.

CALLS FOR UNITY AMONG THE REGIONS

The persistent calls for unity among the diverse regions of Ogun State form a central theme in the ongoing narrative of its political evolution. Chapter 5 delves into this intricate web of aspirations, examining the genuine calls for collaboration and the underlying motivations that drive such appeals. Against a historical backdrop of political disparities and marginalization, this exploration critically analyses the efforts to build bridges that span regional divides.

Within the confines of this discourse, the chapter unravels the multifaceted dynamics, strategies, and challenges associated with the calls for unity, aiming to discern whether these overtures are sincere endeavours or merely political posturing.

To comprehend the significance of the calls for unity, it is essential to trace the historical roots of political disparity in Ogun State. From the early post-independence era, power dynamics began shaping the political landscape, leading to persistent imbalances.

Understanding this historical context provides a lens through which the contemporary calls for unity can be examined, dissecting whether they represent genuine attempts to redress historical wrongs or mere rhetorical gestures.

As political chess pieces move across the board, leaders and activists articulate the need for unity among Ogun State's regions. The chapter navigates through speeches, policy proposals, and collaborative initiatives, scrutinizing the motives behind these calls. Are they driven by a sincere desire to foster a united front for the betterment of the state, or do they conceal strategic manoeuvres that serve narrower interests? This critical analysis aims to decipher the authenticity of these appeals against the backdrop of a historical narrative fraught with political complexities.

Various strategies have been proposed to bridge the political gap in response to the historical disparities. The chapter dissects these strategies, ranging from policy frameworks to collaborative governance models. Leaders and activists from different regions present blueprints for inclusive development, aiming to address the systemic challenges that have perpetuated regional imbalances. The effectiveness of these strategies is scrutinised, emphasising their potential to usher in a new era of unity and collective progress.

Calls for unity are not without challenges, and Chapter 5 delves into the intricacies of these impediments—political manoeuvring, hidden agendas, and historical grievances surface as potential stumbling blocks to genuine collaboration. The chapter exposes the undercurrents that may undermine sincere efforts, offering a nuanced perspective on the complexities inherent in fostering unity among regions with divergent historical experiences.

Embedded within the broader narrative is the voices of the people—those at the grassroots level who bear the direct consequences of regional disparities. Chapter 5 amplifies these voices, providing a platform for community leaders, activists, and everyday citizens to express their perspectives on the calls for unity. Their narratives serve as a poignant reminder of the tangible impact that regional politics has on the lives of individuals and communities.

The chapter delves into past collaborative initiatives to gauge the sincerity of contemporary calls for unity. Case studies of previous attempts at cross-regional cooperation are scrutinized for lessons learned and pitfalls to avoid. This retrospective analysis offers insights into the challenges that have historically impeded unity and informs the present discourse on the road to collaboration.

As the chapter unfolds, it seeks to distil a blueprint for unity—a roadmap that transcends political rhetoric and reflects a genuine commitment to inclusivity. Strategies prioritising equitable resource allocation, transparent governance, and collaborative decision-making emerge as critical components of this blueprint. The vision is one where the diverse regions of Ogun State unite for the collective prosperity of all, leaving behind the shadows of historical disparity.

The chapter sheds light on grassroots movements and activism as catalysts for change. Initiatives driven by the people, advocating for unity and inclusive development, emerge as forces that can reshape the political landscape. Grassroots perspectives are integral to the discourse, offering a ground-level view of the challenges faced by marginalized communities and their aspirations for a more united Ogun State.

Leadership plays a pivotal role in shaping the discourse on unity. Chapter 5 scrutinizes the actions and pronouncements of political leaders, assessing whether their rhetoric aligns with tangible efforts to bridge divides. The chapter delves into the responsibilities of leaders in fostering an environment conducive to collaboration, evaluating their role in transcending historical grievances and steering the state toward a collective future.

Beyond politics, the chapter explores cultural integration and shared identity as potential sources of unity. Cultural initiatives, community dialogues, and efforts to celebrate the rich diversity of Ogun State emerge as avenues through which shared identity can be cultivated. This broader perspective recognizes unity as a political imperative and an intrinsic aspect of the state's social fabric.

Building trust is paramount in the journey toward unity. Transparent governance emerges as an imperative, fostering an environment where citizens can trust that collaborative initiatives are genuine and will result in tangible benefits for all regions. Overcoming scepticism requires a commitment to accountability, openness, and a departure from historical patterns of opaque governance.

As Chapter 5 unfolds, it culminates in a call to action. The discourse on unity extends beyond rhetoric to a tangible commitment to charting the course for a united Ogun State. The chapter challenges readers, leaders, and activists to contribute actively to the transformative journey, emphasizing that building bridges requires collective effort, commitment, and an unwavering dedication to overcoming the challenges that have historically divided the regions.

In traversing the landscape of calls for unity among Ogun State's regions, Chapter 5 emerges as a critical juncture in the narrative—a nuanced exploration of the dynamics, strategies, and challenges inherent in the quest for a more united and harmonious political landscape. The journey through these pages invites readers to engage critically with the complexities of regional politics, envisioning a future where unity prevails over division and collaboration becomes the cornerstone of Ogun State's collective progress.

STRATEGIES TO BRIDGE THE POLITICAL GAP AND PROMOTE INCLUSIVITY

Chapter 5 delves into the heart of Ogun State's political landscape, where the imperative of unity and inclusivity becomes a rallying cry against historical disparities. This chapter meticulously examines the multifaceted strategies proposed to bridge the political gap among the regions, unravelling the complexities of fostering inclusivity. As the narratives unfold, the discourse traverses beyond political rhetoric, scrutinizing the sincerity of these strategies and their potential to reshape the contours of Ogun State's political future.

The formulation of policy frameworks that prioritise equitable resource allocation is at the forefront of strategies to bridge the political gap. The chapter dissects proposals and initiatives that seek to redefine budgetary allocations, ensuring that each region receives a fair share of resources for development. This strategic approach aims to rectify historical imbalances by redirecting resources to neglected regions, fostering a more inclusive development agenda.

Collaborative governance models emerge as another critical strategy, envisioning a paradigm shift from unilateral decision-making to inclusive decision processes. This entails actively involving representatives from diverse regions in policy formulation and implementation. By establishing mechanisms for collaboration, leaders aspire to create a more democratic and representative political structure where the diverse voices of Ogun State find resonance in the corridors of power.

Recognizing the importance of grassroots perspectives, the chapter explores strategies centred on empowerment and community development initiatives. These efforts aim to uplift marginalized communities, addressing socio-economic disparities perpetuating political imbalances. The discourse navigates through specific programs and initiatives designed to enhance education, healthcare, and infrastructure at the grassroots level, fostering an environment where every region can thrive.

A commitment to transparent decision-making processes stands out as a cornerstone strategy. Leaders propose mechanisms to enhance transparency in governance, ensuring that decisions related to resource allocation, development projects, and political appointments are communicated openly. The goal is to build trust among the diverse regions, dispelling scepticism and fostering a sense of collective ownership in the decision-making processes that shape Ogun State's future.

The chapter critically assesses strategies for reassessing electoral boundaries, aiming to rectify gerrymandering and ensure fair representation. Proposals for transparent and unbiased delineation of constituencies form part of this strategy. By revisiting electoral boundaries, leaders seek to dismantle historical structures that have favoured certain regions at the expense of others, fostering a political landscape where each vote carries equal weight.

Education emerges as a critical arena for promoting inclusivity, and the chapter explores strategies related to inclusive educational policies. Leaders envision policies' addressing educational disparities among regions, ensuring every community has access to quality education. This strategic approach aims to bridge the educational gap and cultivate an informed citizenry capable of actively participating in the political process.

The discourse navigates through proposals for cross-regional infrastructure development projects, envisioning initiatives that transcend regional boundaries. Leaders aspire to foster a sense of interconnectedness and shared progress by investing in projects that benefit multiple regions simultaneously. This strategy aims to counteract historical patterns of development favouring specific regions, redirecting infrastructure investments to areas that have long been neglected.

Recognizing the importance of diverse voices, strategies for empowering women and minority groups are scrutinized. Initiatives that ensure the active participation of women and minority leaders in political processes and governance are explored. By fostering inclusivity at every level, these strategies aim to create a political landscape that reflects the diversity of Ogun State's population, breaking down barriers that have historically hindered certain groups from full participation.

The chapter delves into strategies involving civic education and awareness campaigns as vehicles for promoting inclusivity. Leaders propose initiatives to enhance public awareness of political processes, civic responsibilities, and the importance of active participation. By fostering a politically informed citizenry, these strategies aim to overcome historical apathy and empower individuals to engage meaningfully in shaping the political destiny of Ogun State.

Collaboration with non-governmental organizations (NGOs) emerges as a complementary strategy, leveraging external expertise and resources to promote inclusivity. The discourse explores partnerships with NGOs focused on human rights, social justice, and community development. Through collaboration, leaders envision a synergistic approach that supplements governmental efforts, addressing gaps and catalyzing positive change.

Beyond politics, the chapter scrutinizes strategies related to cultural integration initiatives. Efforts to celebrate and preserve the rich cultural diversity of Ogun State form part of this strategic approach. By recognizing and valuing cultural differences, leaders aim to foster a sense of unity that transcends political divides, creating a shared identity that binds the diverse regions together.

Continuous dialogue and conflict resolution mechanisms are explored as essential components of strategies to bridge the political gap. The chapter examines proposals for forums, councils, or commissions fostering open regional dialogue. Leaders aspire to address historical grievances and pave the way for a more harmonious political coexistence by providing platforms for constructive conversations and conflict resolution.

Accountability measures are crucial elements of proposed strategies in the quest for inclusivity. Leaders advocate for mechanisms that ensure accountability in governance, including oversight bodies, independent audits, and public reporting. The goal is to instil confidence in the populace that resources are allocated fairly, development projects are implemented equitably, and political decisions are made transparently.

The discourse amplifies the role of grassroots movements as agents of change, exploring strategies that empower communities to advocate for inclusivity. Grassroots activism, community mobilization, and civic engagement initiatives become instrumental in dismantling historical barriers. The chapter evaluates the potential of grassroots movements to serve as catalysts for political transformation, ensuring that marginalised voices are heard and heeded.

As the chapter unfolds, it confronts the challenges embedded in these strategies. Hidden agendas, political manoeuvring, and historical scepticism are potential hurdles to genuine inclusivity. The discourse navigates through the complexities, offering insights into how leaders can navigate these challenges and build a foundation of trust that transcends historical grievances.

The discourse concludes with a discussion on measuring the success of these strategies. Leaders propose inclusivity metrics, encompassing improved socio-economic conditions in marginalized regions, increased political representation, and enhanced civic participation. By establishing tangible benchmarks, leaders aspire to demonstrate the efficacy of these strategies in reshaping Ogun State's political lands cape. In unravelling the strategies to bridge the political gap and promote inclusivity, Chapter 5 emerges as a critical juncture in the narrative—a comprehensive exploration of the mechanisms that hold the potential to reshape the political destiny of Ogun State. The journey through these pages invites readers to critically engage with the proposed strategies, envisioning a future where unity prevails, inclusivity thrives, and every region contributes to the collective prosperity of Ogun State.

EFFORTS BY ACTIVISTS AND LEADERS TO ADDRESS MARGINALIZATION

In the intricate tapestry of Ogun State's political landscape, Chapter 5 unfurls a narrative that transcends mere rhetoric, delving into the tangible efforts made by activists and leaders to address historical marginalization. This chapter serves as a compass, navigating the initiatives, movements, and strategies wielded by those on the frontline of change. As the narratives unfold, readers are immersed in the stories of resilience, courage, and determination exhibited by activists and leaders striving to dismantle the walls of marginalization and forge a path towards a more equitable Ogun State.

The chapter begins with exploring activists who stand as vanguard voices against marginalization. These individuals, often emerging from marginalized communities themselves, become the embodiment of resilience and advocacy. The discourse navigates through the stories of activists who have fearlessly spoken out against inequity, serving as catalysts for broader movements demanding justice, representation, and inclusivity.

At the grassroots level, movements germinate— organic expressions of communal resilience against marginalization. Chapter 5 illuminates the grassroots movements that burge within communities, led by individuals committed to addressing historical wrongs. These movements become pivotal agents of change, channelling marginalised regions' collective frustrations and aspirations into organized efforts for political transformation.

Efforts to address marginalization pivot on the advocacy for genuine representation. Leaders and activists champion the cause of ensuring that every region within Ogun State is proportionally represented in governance structures. The chapter scrutinizes concrete steps taken to translate advocacy into action, with leaders pushing for policies and electoral reforms that guarantee equitable representation at all levels of government.

The discourse delves into legal battles waged by activists to challenge systemic injustices perpetuating marginalization. Lawsuits become weapons in the fight for equity, with activists strategically utilizing legal avenues to challenge gerrymandering, electoral manipulations, and discriminatory policies. These legal endeavours not only seek justice for past wrongs but also aim to establish precedents that dismantle the structural foundations of marginalization.

Recognizing the intricate link between economic disparity and political marginalization, leaders and activists initiate economic empowerment programs. Chapter 5 navigates through these initiatives, exploring how economic empowerment becomes a potent tool for breaking the chains of poverty that have disproportionately affected certain regions. Entrepreneurs, cooperatives, and skill development programs emerge as avenues for fostering economic self-sufficiency.

Efforts to address marginalization extend to education, where activists and leaders champion educational reforms as a gateway to empowerment. The discourse dissects policies aimed at improving educational infrastructure, increasing access to quality education in marginalized regions, and fostering an environment where every child, regardless of geographical location, has equal opportunities for learning and growth.

Strategic political alliances become a linchpin in the efforts to address marginalization. Activists and leaders recognize the power of unifying regional voices to effect change. The chapter explores how alliances are forged, transcending regional divides to create a formidable front against marginalization. These alliances become crucial in reshaping the political landscape and garnering broader support for the cause of equity.

The chapter unfolds narratives of public awareness campaigns orchestrated by activists and leaders. These campaigns serve as a means to illuminate the shadows of historical marginalization, fostering a broader understanding of the systemic challenges faced by specific regions. Through media, community engagements, and educational programs, activists endeavour to awaken a collective consciousness that challenges the status quo.

Leaders and activists employ grassroots consultations as a strategy for inclusive decision-making. The discourse navigates through instances where leaders actively seek community input, ensuring that the decisions that shape their destinies are made collaboratively. Grassroots consultations become a conduit for expressing the aspirations, concerns, and visions of communities that have long been marginalized.

Youth empowerment emerges as a transformative strategy employed by activists and leaders. The chapter scrutinizes initiatives designed to empower young individuals from marginalized regions, recognizing them as catalysts for change. Educational scholarships, mentorship programs, and youth engagement initiatives become avenues for nurturing a new generation of leaders equipped to challenge and reshape the political narrative.

The global stage becomes a platform for activists and leaders to collaborate with international organizations. Chapter 5 explores how partnerships with entities committed to human rights, social justice, and equitable governance amplify the cause of addressing marginalization. These collaborations leverage international support to bring attention to the struggles faced by marginalized regions within Ogun State.

Efforts to address marginalization extend beyond the political realm to cultural initiatives.

Leaders and activists champion the celebration and preservation of cultural diversity. The discourse navigates through events, festivals, and cultural programs that reclaim and celebrate the unique identities of marginalized regions, fostering a sense of pride and solidarity.

Activists and leaders engage in policy advocacy for infrastructural development, transforming landscapes that have long been neglected. The chapter explores how strategic policies are proposed and implemented to address infrastructural disparities, ensuring that basic amenities, such as roads, healthcare facilities, and utilities, are extended to marginalized regions.

As the narratives unfold, the chapter confronts setbacks—challenges that activists and leaders encounter in their pursuit of addressing marginalization. Hidden opposition, political resistance, and systemic barriers emerge as formidable hurdles. However, the discourse emphasizes the resilience these leaders and activists exhibit, who navigate setbacks with determination, learning from each challenge and adapting strategies for greater efficacy.

The discourse concludes with an assessment of the impact of these efforts. Activists and leaders measure success in rhetoric and tangible change—a transformed political landscape where the shadows of marginalization dissipate. The chapter evaluates indicators such as improved political representation, enhanced socio-economic conditions, and increased civic engagement as metrics of the transformative impact of these collective endeavours.

In traversing the landscape of efforts by activists and leaders to address marginalization,

Chapter 5 emerges as a poignant exploration—a testament to the indomitable spirit of those who refuse to be silenced by historical injustices. The journey through these narratives invites readers to witness the transformative potential of collective action, where activists and leaders become architects of a more equitable and just Ogun State.

CHALLENGES AND ROADBLOCKS IN THE PURSUIT OF UNITY

Chapter 5 unfolds a narrative that confronts the efforts to bridge political gaps and the formidable challenges and roadblocks embedded in the pursuit of unity. As the discourse navigates through the complexities of Ogun State's political landscape, it unravels the multifaceted challenges that activists, leaders, and the populace encounter on the path to fostering unity. These challenges, often deeply rooted in historical grievances and systemic complexities, become pivotal elements in shaping the narrative of Ogun State's quest for a more united and inclusive future.

At the heart of the challenges lies the weight of historical grievances and deep-seated Mistrust among the regions. The chapter delves into the complexities of navigating a political landscape scarred by past injustices. The historical context, marked by disparities in resource allocation, political representation, and development, casts a long shadow over the pursuit of unity. Fuelled by years of perceived marginalization, Mistrust becomes a formidable roadblock that activists and leaders must navigate.

As activists and leaders strive to redefine the political landscape, they encounter resistance from entrenched power structures. The discourse scrutinizes how those who have historically benefited from the status quo may resist efforts to redistribute power and resources more equitably. Entrenched interests, vested in maintaining the existing power dynamics, present formidable challenges that demand strategic navigation.

The chapter explores the challenges of political manoeuvring and opportunism in the pursuit of unity. The intricate chessboard of politics in Ogun State is marked by individuals and factions seeking to exploit the quest for unity for personal gain. The discourse navigates through instances where the noble pursuit of unity becomes entangled in opportunistic agendas, necessitating vigilant leadership to safeguard against manipulation.

Unity efforts encounter challenges stemming from concerns about regional identity and autonomy. The discourse delves into how some regions may harbour fears of losing their unique identity or autonomy in pursuing a more unified Ogun State. Balancing the aspirations for unity with the need to respect and preserve regional identities becomes a delicate challenge that leaders and activists must address to build a shared vision.

Socio-economic disparities, deeply rooted in historical marginalization, present roadblocks in the quest for unity. The chapter scrutinizes how certain regions, burdened by economic neglect, may resist unity efforts if the perception persists that their grievances must be adequately addressed. Bridging socio-economic gaps becomes a challenge and a prerequisite for fostering a sense of collective purpose.

Efforts to foster unity encounter challenges related to the need for inclusive governance structures. The discourse navigates through the complexities of political systems that may not adequately represent the diversity of Ogun State. The absence of mechanisms ensuring equitable representation can impede the effectiveness of unity efforts, necessitating comprehensive reforms to governance structures.

The pursuit of unity is not isolated from external influences and interference. The chapter explores how external factors, whether from neighbouring states, national politics, or international entities, can impact Ogun State's quest for unity. The delicate balance of navigating regional interests amid external pressures becomes a challenging terrain that leaders must navigate with strategic acumen.

The discourse scrutinizes challenges arising from resistance to policy reforms. Policies aimed at rectifying historical imbalances and promoting unity may face resistance from those who perceive such reforms as threats to their interests. The chapter delves into the complexities of overcoming resistance to legislative changes and policy initiatives that form integral components of the unity agenda.

Political fragmentation and factionalism within regions present formidable challenges to unity efforts. The discourse navigates through instances where internal divisions and regional power struggles hinder a cohesive approach to unity. Navigating the intricacies of factionalism becomes a critical aspect of leadership, requiring strategic engagement to align disparate interests.

The pursuit of unity is intricately tied to public perception and scepticism. The chapter explores how the populace, influenced by historical experiences and current realities, may harbour scepticism about the feasibility of unity efforts. Shifting public perception becomes a nuanced challenge, requiring transparent communication, tangible outcomes, and consistent efforts to build trust.

Disputes over resource allocation and economic interests become significant roadblocks in pursuing unity. The discourse delves into how regions, fuelled by concerns over economic benefits, may dispute resource allocation. Addressing these disputes requires a delicate balance that ensures equitable distribution while fostering a shared commitment to the greater good.

The chapter navigates the challenges of balancing regional development priorities within the broader unity framework. Leaders must address the intricacies of allocating resources in a way that respects the unique needs of each region while fostering collective progress. The challenge lies in achieving a harmonious balance that prevents the marginalization of any region in the pursuit of broader unity.

Unity efforts encounter challenges related to resistance to cultural integration initiatives. The discourse explores instances where efforts to celebrate and integrate diverse cultures may face resistance from those who perceive such initiatives as attempts to homogenize unique identities. Leaders must navigate the delicate terrain of fostering unity without erasing the rich tapestry of cultural diversity.

The legacy of past electoral manipulations poses challenges to unity efforts. The chapter delves into how distrust stemming from previous electoral manipulations may linger, hindering the credibility of future electoral processes. Addressing this legacy requires comprehensive electoral reforms and transparent mechanisms to restore confidence in the democratic process.

Managing the expectations of diverse regions amid the complex realities of political reform becomes a central challenge. The discourse navigates through instances where unrealistic expectations may lead to disillusionment. Leaders and activists must effectively communicate the incremental nature of progress while sustaining momentum for transformative change.

Securing genuine cross-regional collaboration proves to be a nuanced challenge. The discourse scrutinizes how leaders must navigate power dynamics and historical dynamics to foster authentic collaboration. Building trust and dismantling preconceived notions become imperative in ensuring that collaboration is symbolic and translates into tangible outcomes.

As Chapter 5 unfolds, readers are immersed in a narrative confronting these challenges and roadblocks head-on. Pursuing unity in Ogun State is a complex journey, requiring astute leadership, strategic navigation, and a collective commitment to transcending historical divides. The discourse invites readers to grapple with the intricacies of these challenges, recognizing that the path to unity is not a linear trajectory but a nuanced exploration of resilience and transformation in the face of formidable obstacles.

Chapter 5, "Building Bridges or Erecting Walls: The Road to Unity," explores the multifaceted journey towards a united and equitable Ogun State. Calls for unity, strategies to bridge the political gap, and efforts by activists and leaders to address marginalization paint a picture of resilience and hope in the face of historical challenges.

The exploration of proposed and implemented initiatives underscores the agency of individuals and communities in shaping the trajectory of Ogun State's political landscape. However, the road to unity is fraught with challenges, and overcoming deep-seated grievances and resistance from established power centres requires sustained commitment and strategic navigation.

As we transition to subsequent chapters, the narrative will continue to unfold, delving into the responses to these challenges and the evolving dynamics of political chess within Ogun State. The voices advocating for justice, equity, and unity persist, echoing the aspirations of a people determined to shape a future where the walls of marginalization are dismantled, and bridges of unity stand tall.

CHAPTER 6

"ECONOMIC FALLOUT: THE COST OF MARGINALIZATION"

In the following pages, Chapter 6 unveils the economic narrative entrenched in the heart of Ogun West—a region marked by the enduring shadows of systemic marginalization. Aptly titled "Economic Fallout: The Cost of Marginalization," this chapter explores the tangible consequences borne by the people and the economic landscape of Ogun West.

As the chapter unfolds, the narrative transcends mere economic analysis; it becomes a profound journey into the lived experiences of a community long relegated to the fringes of development. From crumbling infrastructure to educational inequities, healthcare challenges, and business stagnation, the economic fallout emerges as a compelling narrative that encapsulates the multifaceted impact of historical neglect.

Beyond statistics and theoretical frameworks, the chapter invites readers to witness the economic struggles faced by the residents of

Ogun West, reflecting not only the past but the present and future aspirations of a region seeking to overcome the chains of marginalization. The story unfolds as one of resilience, untapped potential, and a collective determination to redefine the economic trajectory of Ogun West within the broader context of Ogun State.

EXAMINATION OF THE ECONOMIC CONSEQUENCES OF OGUN WEST'S MARGINALIZATION

Ogun West's economic landscape, a region in the southwestern part of Nigeria, bears the indelible marks of historical marginalization. This examination delves deep into the multifaceted consequences that have reverberated through the economic fabric of Ogun West, transcending statistics to unveil the lived experiences of a community grappling with the tangible fallout of systemic neglect.

The economic fallout from marginalization is conspicuously manifested in the glaring disparities in infrastructure development. Roads with yawning potholes, crumbling bridges, and a lack of essential public utilities characterize Ogun West's landscape. The consequence is not merely an inconvenience for residents but a tangible impediment to economic activities. Hindered transportation and connectivity hamper trade and commerce, perpetuating a cycle of economic underdevelopment.

The lack of adequate infrastructure stifles local businesses and discourages potential investors. The economic fallout extends beyond the immediate inconveniences as the region struggles to attract the investments necessary for infrastructure development and economic growth. The consequence is a palpable stagnation, with the potential for economic prosperity hindered by the inadequacies of the physical infrastructure.

Education, as a cornerstone of economic empowerment, examines the consequences of marginalization in Ogun West. The region grapples with a stark disparity in access to quality education. Limited educational resources and a dearth of higher learning institutions hinder Ogun West's intellectual capital. The economic fallout is not just a lack of educational opportunities but a perpetuation of cycles of poverty and underdevelopment.

The consequence of educational inequities extends beyond individual lives to impact the region's overall economic trajectory. A workforce with limited access to quality education hampers the development of knowledge-based economic sectors. Ogun West is thus denied the opportunity to contribute significantly to industries that require a well-educated and skilled workforce, perpetuating a cycle of economic disadvantage.

Marginalization manifests prominently in the healthcare sector, where Ogun West grapples with challenges in accessing quality healthcare services. Insufficient healthcare infrastructure and limited medical facilities result in compromised resident health outcomes. The economic fallout is twofold—impaired productivity due to health issues and the economic burden of treating preventable illnesses.

The consequences of healthcare challenges are profound, affecting both individual well-being and the region's economic productivity. Preventable illnesses, left untreated due to inadequate healthcare facilities, lead to a workforce with compromised health, hindering its capacity to contribute meaningfully to economic activities. The economic fallout is thus not confined to the realm of healthcare but extends its tendrils into the broader economic landscape of Ogun West.

Agriculture, often the backbone of regional economies, is prominent in examining the economic consequences of marginalization in Ogun West. The region needs more support, outdated farming techniques, and inadequate infrastructure, all hindering agricultural productivity. The economic fallout extends beyond the farming community to impact food security and the income-generating potential of the agricultural sector.

The consequences of these agricultural implications are far-reaching. Ogun West, endowed with fertile land and agricultural potential, finds its economic growth stunted by the need for more support and infrastructure. The potential for agriculture to drive economic development is curtailed, perpetuating a cycle of dependence on less sustainable economic activities. The economic fallout thus becomes a collective hindrance to the region's overall economic prosperity.

Marginalization translates into high unemployment rates in Ogun West. The region needs more industries, investment, and job opportunities, leading to a stagnation of economic growth. Human capital must be utilised more, hindering personal and regional economic development.

The economic fallout from employment challenges goes beyond individual struggles to the broader economic landscape. Ogun West, deprived of industries and job opportunities, faces a stagnant economy with limited avenues for income generation. The consequence is a lack of employment and a systemic hindrance to the region's ability to harness its human resources for economic growth and development.

The economic fallout of marginalization is palpable in the stagnation of businesses within Ogun West. The absence of a conducive business environment, inadequate infrastructure, and limited market access stifles entrepreneurial ventures. The consequence is a region deprived of the vibrant economic activity that could propel it towards prosperity.

Business stagnation becomes a cyclical challenge for Ogun West, as the lack of economic vibrancy hinders the growth and sustainability of local enterprises. The consequence is a diminished capacity for wealth creation, job generation, and overall economic dynamism. The economic fallout thus permeates the business landscape, restricting the potential for economic prosperity within the region.

The erosion of economic confidence emerges as a consequence of historical neglect. Ogun West grapples with a need for more investor confidence, inhibiting external investments and local initiatives. The economic fallout is the absence of monetary influx and a pervasive sentiment of economic despondency, hindering local economic initiatives.

The consequence of eroded economic confidence is a self-perpetuating cycle of economic stagnation. The region, lacking the necessary investments and confidence in its economic potential, struggles to break free from the shackles of marginalization. The economic fallout becomes a psychological barrier, impeding the region's ability to attract investments, foster local initiatives, and propel economic growth.

Marginalization affects not only conventional economic sectors but also cultural industries. The stifling of cultural entrepreneurship and limited promotion of indigenous arts result in an untapped economic potential within the creative sector. The economic fallout extends to the region's cultural economy, hindering artistic and creative expression opportunities.

Often overlooked in economic analyses, cultural industries become a casualty of marginalization. The consequence is a loss of cultural diversity and a missed economic opportunity. Ogun West, rich in cultural heritage, faces an economic fallout that extends beyond conventional sectors, impacting the vibrant creative economy that could contribute significantly to the region's overall economic prosperity.

Consequences manifest in the form of unequal access to economic opportunities. Political decisions favouring certain regions result in economic benefits that leave Ogun West on the periphery. The economic fallout is more than just opportunities and a perpetuation of disparities, hindering regional development.

The unequal access to economic opportunities becomes a systemic challenge, perpetuating a cycle of economic disadvantage for Ogun West. The consequence is a need for economic opportunities and a deepening of existing disparities that hinder the region's ability to participate fully in the broader economic landscape. The economic fallout becomes a barrier to inclusive and sustainable regional development.

The examination reveals a developmental lag experienced by Ogun West, necessitating economic catch-up. Overcoming systemic barriers to development becomes an uphill journey, requiring concerted efforts to bridge the gap created by historical neglect.

The consequence of developmental lag is a region grappling with the challenges of catching up with more economically privileged counterparts. Ogun West, burdened by the economic fallout of marginalization, faces the herculean task of overcoming historical barriers to development. The consequence is not merely a current state of underdevelopment but the uphill journey required to establish a more equitable and sustainable economic trajectory.

In conclusion, examining the economic consequences of Ogun West's marginalization reveals a complex interplay of challenges that have hindered the region's economic prosperity. From infrastructure disparities to educational inequities, healthcare challenges, and business stagnation, the economic fallout becomes a collective struggle for a community determined to break free from the chains of historical neglect. The story that unfolds is not one of resignation but a resilient call to action, urging stakeholders to envision and work towards a future where Ogun West's economic vibrancy contributes significantly to the collective prosperity of Ogun State.

THE POTENTIAL FOR ECONOMIC GROWTH THROUGH REGIONAL COLLABORATION

The prospect of economic growth is often intricately tied to collaboration, especially within the regional context. In the case of Ogun State, where historical marginalization has cast a shadow over its developmental trajectory, exploring the potential for economic growth through regional collaboration becomes both a necessity and a beacon of hope. This discourse delves into the multifaceted dimensions of regional collaboration and how fostering partnerships among diverse regions within Ogun State can unlock untapped economic opportunities.

Regional collaboration inherently carries the promise of strength in unity. By fostering collaboration among the diverse regions of Ogun State, namely Ogun Central, Ogun East, and Ogun West, each region's collective strengths and resources can be harnessed for mutual benefit. A united front can amplify the impact of initiatives, creating a more robust foundation for economic growth. This synergy becomes a powerful antidote to the historical divisions that have hindered collective progress.

Pooling resources for infrastructure development is a pivotal aspect of regional collaboration. Investing in shared infrastructure projects that benefit all regions can gradually address the economic fallout from historical neglect. Roads, bridges, and utilities connecting various regions facilitate smoother economic activities and foster a sense of interdependence. This shared investment in infrastructure becomes a catalyst for economic growth, laying the groundwork for improved transportation, trade, and connectivity.

Each region within Ogun State possesses unique economic strengths and specializations. With its proximity to economic hubs like Lagos, Ogun Central may excel in commerce and trade. Ogun East, endowed with agricultural resources, may contribute significantly to agribusiness. Despite historical marginalization, Ogun West might have untapped potential in cultural and creative industries. Regional collaboration allows for the strategic leveraging of these diverse economic specializations. A more balanced and diversified economy can emerge by recognizing and capitalizing on each region's strengths.

As a common thread across Ogun State's regions, agriculture presents a ripe opportunity for collaborative efforts. Integrating the agribusiness value chain, from production to processing and distribution, can be a transformative strategy. Ogun East, known for its agricultural abundance, can focus on cultivation, while Ogun Central and West can contribute to processing and distribution. This integrated approach boosts the agricultural sector and creates a ripple effect across the broader economy, generating employment and fostering economic resilience.

Collaboration in the realms of education and technology holds immense potential. By establishing knowledge exchange programs and collaborative research initiatives, each region can benefit from the educational and technological advancements of the others. With its proximity to educational institutions and tech hubs, Ogun Central can play a pivotal role in driving this exchange. The result is a more educated and skilled workforce across the state, capable of contributing to innovation and technological advancements that fuel economic growth.

Ogun State boasts a rich cultural heritage and natural attractions across its regions. Collaborative efforts in sustainable tourism development can preserve these assets and drive economic growth. Ogun East's natural landscapes, Ogun Central's historical sites, and Ogun West's cultural heritage can collectively form a diverse tourism portfolio. Regional collaboration in marketing and infrastructure development can transform the state into a sought-after tourist destination, generating revenue and employment opportunities.

Industrialization, a key driver of economic growth, can be approached collectively through regional collaboration. Each region can identify and develop specific industries based on their strengths. With its commercial prowess, Ogun Central can serve as a trading and manufacturing hub. With its agricultural abundance, Ogun East can contribute to food processing industries. By leveraging its cultural assets, Ogun West can explore creative and cultural industries. This collective approach ensures that industrialization is distributed strategically, minimizing regional disparities.

Encouraging cross-regional investment is essential for balanced economic growth. By promoting investment opportunities in each region and facilitating partnerships, the economic potential of Ogun State as a whole can be realized. The economic nerve centre of Ogun Central can attract financial and commercial investments. Ogun East can entice agribusiness and manufacturing investments, while Ogun West can leverage cultural and creative industries. This cross-regional investment promotion creates a more inclusive and dynamic economic landscape.

Collaborative skill development initiatives can address the disparities in human capital across regions. With access to educational institutions and training centres, Ogun Central can play a leading role in facilitating skill development programs. By creating a skilled and adaptable workforce, the regions can collectively enhance their competitiveness in various sectors. This collaborative approach ensures that the benefits of skill development are distributed equitably, fostering economic inclusivity.

Harmonizing policies across regions and advocating for equitable governance is crucial for successful regional collaboration. By aligning regulatory frameworks and advocating for policies that promote fairness and inclusivity, the regions can create an environment conducive to economic growth. This collaborative effort extends to engaging with policymakers at the state and national levels to ensure that the concerns and aspirations of each region are heard and addressed.

In conclusion, the potential for economic growth through regional collaboration in Ogun State is vast and transformative. By leveraging each region's collective strengths, resources, and unique economic specializations, Ogun State can move towards a more balanced and resilient economy. This collaborative journey is not just about economic prosperity; it is a collective endeavour to rewrite the narrative of Ogun State, transcending historical divisions and fostering a future where every region contributes significantly to the state's overall development.

Chapter 6, "Economic Fallout: The Cost of Marginalization," delves into the tangible consequences of marginalization on the economic landscape of Ogun West. Disparities in infrastructure development, education, and healthcare paint a vivid picture of the challenges faced by the region. However, amidst these challenges, the potential for economic growth through regional collaboration emerges as a beacon of hope.

Examining economic consequences underscores the urgency of addressing historical imbalances and investing in inclusive development strategies. By fostering collaboration, dismantling barriers, and implementing transformative initiatives, Ogun State can unlock the full economic potential of all its regions.

As the narrative progresses, subsequent chapters will explore the responses to these economic challenges and the evolving dynamics of regional collaboration within Ogun State. The voices advocating for a more inclusive and prosperous future echo the aspirations of a people determined to overcome the economic fallout of marginalization.

CHAPTER 7

"HOPE FOR CHANGE: OGUN WEST'S POLITICAL RENAISSANCE"

C hapter 7 unfolds as a beacon of hope and resurgence in the intricate tapestry of Ogun State's political landscape. Titled "Hope for Change: Ogun West's Political Renaissance," this chapter embarks on a narrative journey that traces the emergence of a new era for Ogun West. The pages of this chapter are filled with stories of resilience, determination, and the unwavering spirit of a community that refuses to be confined by the shadows of historical marginalization.

As we delve into the heart of this chapter, a compelling tale unfolds—one marked by the emergence of new leaders, the stirrings of grassroots movements, and the unyielding pursuit of political representation and equal opportunities. Ogun West, long relegated to the sidelines of political power, is now experiencing a renaissance—a revival Fuelled by the collective aspirations of a people determined to reclaim their rightful place in the political narrative of Ogun State.

The narrative is not just about political manoeuvring; it is a testament to the courage of individuals who have stepped into leadership roles with a vision for positive change. Grassroots movements, often the catalysts for political transformation, find their voice as

Ogun West residents unite to advocate for a fair and inclusive political landscape. The chapter explores the nuances of this renaissance, examining the strategies employed, the challenges faced, and the milestones achieved in the quest for political equity.

Economic consequences, the fallout from historical neglect, are scrutinized through the lens of hope and change. As new leaders emerge, the economic potential of Ogun West becomes a focal point, with a vision for a revitalized and thriving region. The chapter unfolds as a testament to a community's resilience that refuses to be defined by its past, envisioning a future where economic prosperity is not just a distant dream but an achievable reality.

Amidst the challenges faced, voices rise from Ogun West—leaders, activists, and ordinary citizens whose struggles echo through the pages. Their stories, often unheard in the cacophony of political discourse, take centre stage. The economic consequences of neglect become a rallying cry for change, and the chapter navigates through the voices that demand attention, understanding, and action.

As the political renaissance gains momentum, the chapter explores the evolving dynamics of power and representation. The quest for equal opportunities is not just a political slogan but a driving force that shapes the strategies, alliances, and political discourse in Ogun West. This chapter challenges existing narratives and invites readers to witness the unfolding of a new era—a chapter where hope, resilience, and political renaissance converge to rewrite the story of Ogun West.

In these pages, readers are invited to witness the dawn of change, where the indomitable spirit of Ogun West refuses to be subdued. "Hope for Change: Ogun West's Political Renaissance" is not just a chapter; it is a testament to the enduring spirit of a community reclaiming its narrative, reshaping its destiny, and inspiring a vision for a united and prosperous Ogun State.

THE EMERGENCE OF NEW LEADERS FROM OGUN WEST

In the political landscape of Ogun West, a transformative narrative is unfolding—one marked by the emergence of new leaders who are reshaping the contours of power, challenging historical marginalization, and becoming catalysts for change. This section explores the dynamic personalities and visionary leaders who have risen from Ogun West, steering the region towards a new era of political engagement, economic revitalization, and social empowerment.

At the forefront of Ogun West's political renaissance are leaders characterized by a clear vision and a resolute sense of purpose. These visionaries recognize the historical disparities and are committed to dismantling the barriers that have hindered the region's progress. Their leadership is rooted in a deep understanding of the challenges faced by Ogun West, coupled with a visionary outlook that transcends immediate obstacles.

The emerging leaders from Ogun West are committed to community-centric governance. Unlike predecessors who may have overlooked the needs of the local population, these new leaders prioritize community development, ensuring that policies and initiatives resonate with the aspirations and challenges of the people they represent. Their leadership is marked by a hands-on approach, engaging with the grassroots and understanding the community's pulse.

A distinguishing feature of the new leaders is their political activism and grassroots mobilization background. Many of them have risen through the ranks, starting as activists advocating for the rights and representation of Ogun West. This grassroots foundation has instilled in them a deep connection to the people and a keen awareness of the issues that matter most to the community.

A progressive shift is noticeable in the emerging leadership, marked by a commitment to gender inclusivity. Women leaders from Ogun West are making strides, breaking barriers, and contributing significantly to the region's political renaissance. This inclusivity is not just symbolic but translates into policies that address gender disparities and empower women to play active roles in the socio-economic development of Ogun West.

Recognizing the demographic landscape of Ogun West, the new leaders are actively engaged in empowering and involving the youth. Initiatives that foster education, skill development, and youth participation in governance are gaining prominence. By investing in the younger generation's potential, these leaders are sowing the seeds for sustained progress and dynamic leadership continuity.

The emerging leaders understand the importance of collaboration within Ogun West and beyond. Strategic alliances with like-minded individuals, organizations, and even political figures from other regions have become instrumental in amplifying their impact. By fostering collaborations, these leaders enhance their collective ability to influence policy, challenge existing power structures, and advocate for Ogun West's rightful place in the broader political landscape.

Beyond political acumen, the new leaders from Ogun West are positioned as economic visionaries. They recognize the region's economic potential and are actively formulating policies to harness and amplify it. Initiatives that encourage entrepreneurship attract investments, and promote sustainable economic development are central to their agenda. Their economic vision extends beyond immediate gains, aiming for long-term prosperity and transcending political cycles.

Social justice is a cornerstone of the leadership emerging from Ogun West. Leaders are vocal advocates for equity, fairness, and eradicating persistent social inequalities. Policies addressing education, healthcare, and infrastructural development are grounded in the principles of social justice, ensuring that progress is inclusive and benefits every stratum of society.

The journey of these new leaders is challenging. Navigating the intricate political landscape of Ogun State, they encounter resistance from established power structures and contend with historical prejudices. However, their ability to navigate these political landmines with resilience and strategic acumen distinguishes them as leaders capable of bringing about substantive change.

Departures from the opacity that may have characterized previous administrations, the new leaders emphasize public accountability and transparency. Open communication, accessibility to constituents, and a commitment to ethical governance define their approach. By fostering trust through transparency, these leaders aim to bridge the gap between the government and the governed.

In conclusion, the emergence of new leaders from Ogun West signifies a paradigm shift—a departure from the status quo towards a more dynamic, inclusive, and forward-looking political landscape. Their leadership is not merely about occupying positions of authority but about steering Ogun West towards a future defined by progress, representation, and resilience. As catalysts for change, these leaders embody the aspirations of a community poised to reclaim its narrative and shape a destiny marked by prosperity, unity, and equitable political representation.

GRASSROOTS MOVEMENTS AND POLITICAL ACTIVISM

In the annals of Ogun West's political history, grassroots movements and political activism have emerged as potent forces of change, challenging the status quo and advocating for the region's rights, representation, and equitable development. This section delves into the dynamic landscape of grassroots movements and political activism within Ogun West, examining their historical roots, key players, strategies employed, and the transformative impact on the region's political trajectory.

The roots of grassroots movements in Ogun West can be traced back to the historical marginalization faced by the region. Systematic neglect in infrastructure, economic opportunities, and political representation Fuelled discontent among the local population.

Grassroots movements emerged as a natural response to these historical injustices, serving as catalysts for mobilization and change.

At the core of grassroots movements in Ogun West are community-led initiatives driven by ordinary citizens determined to make a difference. These initiatives often start at the local level, addressing immediate concerns and laying the groundwork for broader advocacy. Whether it is advocating for improved infrastructure, educational facilities, or healthcare services, community-led movements focus on issues that directly impact the lives of residents.

Grassroots movements in Ogun West are distinguished by their reliance on leaders emerging from within the community. These leaders are not imported from external sources but are individuals deeply rooted in the local fabric, intimately acquainted with the struggles faced by their fellow residents. This internal leadership dynamic fosters a genuine connection with the grassroots, ensuring that advocacy aligns with the authentic needs of the people.

Political activism in Ogun West has often centred around the core demand for increased political representation. Grassroots movements advocate for a more inclusive political landscape where the region's interests are considered and actively represented. This advocacy extends to local and state-level politics, challenging the historical underrepresentation of Ogun West in key decision-making bodies.

The youth, recognizing their pivotal role in shaping the future, have played a significant part in grassroots movements. Empowerment initiatives, educational programs, and platforms for youth engagement are integral to these movements. By involving the younger generation, grassroots activists ensure the continuity of their advocacy and inject fresh perspectives into the discourse surrounding Ogun West's development.

Grassroots movements in Ogun West understand the importance of forging strategic alliances and networking. Collaborations with like-minded organizations, activists, and even sympathetic political figures from other regions amplify the impact of their advocacy. This networking strategy broadens the reach of grassroots movements, creating a united front against historical marginalization.

In the contemporary landscape, grassroots movements leverage traditional and social media platforms to amplify their voices.

Campaigns, awareness drives, and updates on advocacy efforts are disseminated through various channels, reaching a wider audience. This media platform utilisation serves as a means of communication and a tool for holding those in power accountable.

Grassroots activism in Ogun West has reverberations in electoral processes. The collective voice of the grassroots often influences political narratives, party manifestos, and candidate selection. By actively participating in electoral processes, these movements aim to ensure that elected representatives align with the aspirations of Ogun West and are committed to addressing historical imbalances.

Grassroots movements exert pressure for policy reforms that address the specific needs of Ogun West. Whether it is advocating for targeted development programs, economic incentives, or social justice initiatives, these movements serve as conduits for channelling the people's aspirations into actionable policy changes. Their advocacy goes beyond rhetoric, seeking tangible reforms that uplift the region.

Grassroots movements in Ogun West exhibit remarkable resilience in the face of challenges. These movements persevere, whether resistance from established power structures, political manoeuvring, or external pressures. This resilience is a testament to the unwavering commitment of grassroots activists to the cause of securing a brighter and more equitable future for Ogun West.

In conclusion, grassroots movements and political activism in Ogun West are testimonials to the indomitable spirit of a community determined to rewrite its narrative. The dynamics of these movements, rooted in historical struggles and propelled by a vision for a better future, are reshaping the political landscape of Ogun West. As the voices from the grassroots grow louder, the impact on political representation, policy reforms, and the overall trajectory of the region becomes increasingly pronounced, marking a pivotal chapter in the ongoing narrative of Ogun West's political evolution.

OGUN WEST'S QUEST FOR POLITICAL REPRESENTATION AND EQUAL OPPORTUNITIES

Ogun West's quest for political representation and equal opportunities is deeply embedded in the region's historical, social, and economic fabric. The narrative unfolds as a poignant tale of a community grappling with systemic marginalization, navigating political complexities, and demanding a rightful place in the broader political discourse of Ogun State.

The historical context of Ogun West's quest is pivotal in understanding the persistent struggle for political representation. The post-independence era witnessed the evolution of political structures in Ogun State, and Ogun West found itself on the sidelines of decision-making processes. The region's geographical location and demographic composition became factors that, rather than being assets, contributed to its marginalization. The absence of adequate representation in political spheres created a longstanding sense of disenfranchisement.

Ogun West's quest is intricately tied to the political landscape of Ogun State, where power dynamics have historically favoured other regions. The rise of Ogun Central in state politics often resulted in the sidelining of Ogun West, leading to a palpable disparity in political influence and representation. Understanding this dynamic is crucial in unravelling the layers of Ogun West's struggle for political relevance.

Leaders and activists from Ogun West have played a pivotal role in articulating the region's aspirations. Their voices echo through grassroots movements, advocacy initiatives, and political activism addressing historical injustices. These leaders, emerging from within the community, bring a nuanced understanding of the challenges faced by Ogun West and advocate for policies that rectify the imbalances.

The quest for political representation is inseparable from the economic implications of neglect. Ogun West seeks equal economic development, infrastructure, education, and healthcare opportunities. Compared to other parts of Ogun State, the region's underdevelopment underscores the economic fallout of historical marginalization. The quest, therefore, extends beyond political offices to encompass broader socio-economic empowerment.

Ogun West's journey has obstacles. The region faces resistance from established power structures, historical prejudices, and the intricate web of political manoeuvring. However, the quest is marked by resilience— resilience to overcome challenges, challenge existing narratives and persist in pursuing political representation and equal opportunities.

Ogun West's quest is not driven by separatism but is a call for inclusivity and unity within Ogun State. The region envisions a future where every part of the state contributes to and benefits from its collective progress. The quest reflects the broader yearning for a political landscape where fairness, justice, and representation are not confined to specific regions but shared across the entire state.

Ogun West's quest for political representation and equal opportunities transcends a desire for political power; it embodies a collective vision for a more just, inclusive, and united Ogun State. The narrative is one of resilience, determination, and a commitment to shaping a political landscape that reflects the aspirations of all its diverse communities.

THE PATH FORWARD: OVERCOMING CHALLENGES AND SEIZING OPPORTUNITIES

Navigating the path forward for Ogun West entails a multifaceted approach that addresses challenges while leveraging opportunities for positive change. This section delves into the intricacies of charting a course that overcomes historical obstacles and seizes the opportunities available for the region's socio-economic and political advancement.

One key strategy for the path forward is cultivating stronger alliances within Ogun State and beyond. Ogun West can seek collaboration with like-minded individuals, organizations, and political figures who share the vision of a more inclusive and equitable state. The region can amplify its voice, garner support, and foster a united front against historical marginalization by forming strategic alliances.

Advocacy for policy reforms remains a crucial aspect of the path forward. Ogun West must actively shape policies that address its specific needs and aspirations. This involves participating in legislative processes, influencing decision-making, and ensuring policies are enacted to bridge the historical gaps in infrastructure, education, healthcare, and economic development.

Recognizing the potential of youth and women as catalysts for change, the path forward involves deliberate efforts to empower these demographics. Initiatives focusing on education, skill development, and entrepreneurship can uplift the younger generation, ensuring they play active roles in Ogun West's socio-economic and political landscape. Similarly, empowering women enhances their contributions to community development and fosters gender-inclusive governance.

Ogun West possesses an untapped economic potential that can be harnessed for the region's development. The path forward involves identifying key sectors—agriculture, commerce, and industry, for example—and implementing strategic plans to maximize economic opportunities. By attracting investments and promoting sustainable development, Ogun West can contribute significantly to the overall prosperity of Ogun State.

Civic education and awareness campaigns are integral to the path forward. Ogun West must embark on initiatives that inform and educate its populace about their rights, the political process, and the importance of active civic participation. This knowledge equips the community to make informed decisions, engage in constructive dialogue, and hold elected officials accountable.

Actively seeking representation in government at various levels is a critical step forward. Ogun West should identify and support capable leaders who represent the region effectively.

This involves participating in electoral processes, supporting candidates with a genuine commitment to Ogun West's development, and ensuring the region is well-represented in decision-making.

Preserving and celebrating the cultural identity of Ogun West is a vital component of the path forward. Embracing cultural heritage fosters a sense of pride and serves as a unifying force. Cultural preservation can be a tool for community cohesion, creating a shared identity that transcends political divisions.

Emphasizing accountability and transparency is crucial for effective governance. The path forward includes advocating for open and transparent governance, where elected officials are accountable to the people. This fosters trust, encourages public participation, and ensures that resources are utilized for the benefit of Ogun West.

The path forward necessitates adaptability to changing political, economic, and social dynamics. Ogun West should remain agile in responding to emerging challenges and opportunities, adjusting strategies to align with evolving circumstances. This adaptability ensures resilience and the ability to navigate the complexities of the political landscape.

Above all, the path forward involves fostering unity and inclusivity within Ogun West and across Ogun State. Embracing diversity, promoting dialogue, and actively seeking common ground contribute to a more cohesive and united front. By transcending historical divisions, Ogun West can work towards a future where all regions of Ogun State thrive collectively.

In conclusion, the path forward for Ogun West is a dynamic and multifaceted journey. Overcoming challenges and seizing opportunities requires a strategic and collaborative approach rooted in the community's aspirations. By actively pursuing these pathways, Ogun West can shape a future marked by progress, representation, and equitable development within the broader context of Ogun State.

Chapter 7, "Hope for Change: Ogun West's Political Renaissance," unravels a narrative of resilience, determination, and hope within Ogun West. The emergence of new leaders, grassroots movements, and political activism signals a renaissance that challenges the entrenched norms of marginalization.

As Ogun West navigates the path toward political representation and equal opportunities, the quest for change encounters obstacles, yet the determination to overcome challenges and seize opportunities for a brighter future prevails. The evolving dynamics within Ogun State's political landscape hint at a potential transformation that transcends historical barriers, laying the foundation for a more inclusive and equitable era.

CONCLUSION

A NEW CHAPTER FOR OGUN STATE POLITICS

In the final pages of "Ogun Central Chess: Unravelling the Political Game and Ogun West's Marginalization," the narrative converges, leaving readers with a profound reflection on the intricate political tapestry of Ogun State. This concluding chapter serves as a compass, guiding us through the labyrinth of historical disparities, power struggles, and the resilient spirit of Ogun West while beckoning towards a future defined by equity and unity.

The journey in the book commenced with an exploration of Ogun State's rich history, geography, and demographics in Chapter 1. It provided the backdrop against which the political consciousness of the state emerged, sowing the seeds for the disparities that unfolded among its regions.

Chapter 2 unfolded the power dynamics within Ogun Central, revealing the rise of influential figures and the strategies employed to maintain and consolidate power. Examining policies favouring Ogun Central underscored the challenges faced by Ogun West in navigating a political landscape that often marginalized its interests.

Chapter 3 illuminated the historical context of Ogun West's contributions to the state, unveiling the systematic marginalization and its far-reaching impact. Voices from Ogun West— leaders, activists, and everyday citizens— painted a vivid picture of neglect, and the economic consequences of this marginalization were laid bare.

Elections and manipulations took centre stage in Chapter 4, where past electoral outcomes were dissected. Ogun Central's role in manipulating these processes perpetuated the marginalization of Ogun West, and specific case studies illustrated the nuances of a political game where fairness seemed elusive.

Amidst the challenges, Chapter 5 resonated with calls for unity among the regions.

Strategies to bridge political gaps and promote inclusivity were explored, showcasing the tireless efforts of activists and leaders to address marginalization collectively.

Chapter 6 delved into the economic fallout resulting from Ogun West's marginalization. Disparities in infrastructure, education, and healthcare were scrutinized, emphasizing the potential for economic growth through regional collaboration.

The emergence of new leaders and grassroots movements from Ogun West took centre stage in Chapter 7. The political renaissance signified a collective quest for representation and equal opportunities, injecting hope into a narrative previously dominated by disparity.

As we conclude, the historical narrative of Ogun State politics is summarized, and the current state of affairs is assessed. The prospects for change are contemplated, and a resounding call for unity echoes. The importance of collaboration becomes evident, transcending regional boundaries for the holistic development of Ogun State.

In this concluding chapter, the epilogue reflects on the potential for a more inclusive and equitable political landscape in Ogun State. It urges citizens to recognize their pivotal role in shaping the state's future, emphasizing the collective responsibility to contribute to a united and prosperous Ogun State. "Ogun Central Chess" concludes not merely as a record of events but as a catalyst for change. It invites readers to reflect on the political intricacies of Ogun State, inspiring a commitment to advocacy and transformative action. The book stands as a testament to the resilience of Ogun West, a plea for justice, and a rallying cry for a united Ogun State where the political game is played on a level field, ensuring every community's rightful place in the shared destiny of the state.